ESPACES

Rendez-vous avec le monde francophone

Cherie Mitschke

Cheryl Tano

VISTA
HIGHER LEARNING

Boston, Massachusetts

ISBN: 978-1-60576-164-0

1 2 3 4 5 6 7 8 9 BB 14 13 12 11 10 09

Table of Contents

Introduction

The ESPACES 2e Lab Manual

Completely coordinated with the **ESPACES** student textbook, the Lab Manual for **ESPACES** provides you with additional practice of the vocabulary, grammar, and language functions presented in each of the textbook's fifteen two-lesson units. The Lab Manual will also help you build your listening and speaking skills in French. The **ressources** boxes in the **ESPACES** textbook indicate where you will find additional practice. Answers to the Lab Manual activities are located in a separate answer key.

The laboratory activities and the **ESPACES** Lab Program MP3s on the **ESPACES** Supersite are meant to work together. Their purpose is to build your listening comprehension, speaking, and pronunciation skills in French, as they reinforce the vocabulary and grammar of the corresponding textbook lesson. The Lab Manual guides you through the Lab MP3 files, providing the printed cues—direction lines, models, charts, drawings, etc.—you need in order to follow along easily. The MP3s contain statements, questions, mini-dialogues, conversations, monologues, commercials, and many other kinds of listening passages, all recorded by native French speakers. In order to keep you engaged, the activities come in a variety of formats, such as listening-and-repeating exercises, listening-and-speaking practice, listening-and-writing activities, illustration-based work, and dictations.

Each laboratory lesson contains a **Espace contextes** section that practices the active vocabulary taught in the corresponding textbook lesson. In most lessons, the **Les sons et les lettres** section parallels the textbook's, and offers a dictation activity. Each laboratory lesson closes with the **Espace structures** section practice.

We hope that you will find the **ESPACES 2e** Lab Manual to be a useful language learning resource that will help you to increase your French language skills.

The ESPACES 2e authors and the Vista Higher Learning Editorial Staff

Unité 1

ESPACE CONTEXTES

Leçon 1A

1 **Identifiez** You will hear six short exchanges. For each one, decide whether it is a greeting, an introduction, or a leave-taking. Mark the appropriate column with an **X**.

> **Modèle**
> *You hear:* **AUDREY** Bonjour, Laura!
> **LAURA** Salut, Audrey. Ça va?
> **AUDREY** Ça va bien, merci. Et toi?
> **LAURA** Pas mal.
> *You mark:* an **X** under *Greeting*

	Greeting	Introduction	Leave-taking
Modèle	X		
1.			
2.			
3.			
4.			
5.			
6.			

2 **Questions** Listen to each question or statement and respond with an answer from the list in your lab manual. Repeat the correct response after the speaker.

a. Enchanté(e).
b. À demain.
c. Je m'appelle Marie.
d. Il n'y a pas de quoi.
e. Comme ci, comme ça. Et toi?
f. Très bien, merci. Et vous?

3 **Associez** You will hear three conversations. Look at the drawings and write the number of the conversation under the appropriate group of people.

a. _____ b. _____ c. _____

LES SONS ET LES LETTRES

The French alphabet

The French alphabet is made up of the same 26 letters as the English alphabet. While they look the same, some letters are pronounced differently. They also sound different when you spell.

lettre	exemple	lettre	exemple	lettre	exemple
a (a)	adresse	j (ji)	justice	s (esse)	spécial
b (bé)	banane	k (ka)	kilomètre	t (té)	table
c (cé)	carotte	l (elle)	lion	u (u)	unique
d (dé)	dessert	m (emme)	mariage	v (vé)	vidéo
e (e)	rebelle	n (enne)	nature	w (double vé)	wagon
f (effe)	fragile	o (o)	olive	x (iks)	xylophone
g (gé)	genre	p (pé)	personne	y (i grec)	yoga
h (hache)	héritage	q (ku)	quiche	z (zède)	zéro
i (i)	innocent	r (erre)	radio		

Notice that some letters in French words have accents. You'll learn how they influence pronunciation in later lessons. Whenever you spell a word in French, include the name of the accent after the letter. For double letters, use **deux** (deux s).

accent	nom	exemple	orthographe
´	*accent aigu*	identité	*I-D-E-N-T-I-T-E-accent aigu*
`	*accent grave*	problème	*P-R-O-B-L-E-accent grave-M-E*
^	*accent circonflexe*	hôpital	*H-O-accent circonflexe-P-I-T-A-L*
¨	*tréma*	naïve	*N-A-I-tréma-V-E*
¸	*cédille*	ça	*C-cédille-A*

1   **L'alphabet** Practice saying the French alphabet and example words aloud.

2   **Ça s'écrit comment?** Spell these words aloud in French.

1. judo	5. existe	9. musique	13. différence
2. yacht	6. clown	10. favorite	14. intelligent
3. forêt	7. numéro	11. kangourou	15. dictionnaire
4. zèbre	8. français	12. parachute	16. alphabet

3   **Dictons** Practice reading these sayings aloud.

     1. Grande invitation, petites portions.   2. Tout est bien qui finit bien.

4   **Dictée** You will hear six people introduce themselves. Listen carefully and write the people's names as they spell them.

1. _____

2. _____

3. _____

4. _____

5. _____

6. _____

ESPACE STRUCTURES

1A.1 Nouns and articles

1 **Identifiez** You will hear a series of words. Decide whether the word is masculine or feminine, and mark the appropriate column with an **X**.

Modèle

You hear: librairie
You mark: an **X** under **Féminin**

	Masculin	Féminin
Modèle	_____	____X____
1.	_____	_____
2.	_____	_____
3.	_____	_____
4.	_____	_____
5.	_____	_____
6.	_____	_____
7.	_____	_____
8.	_____	_____

2 **Changez** Change each word from the masculine to the feminine. Repeat the correct answer after the speaker. (*6 items*)

Modèle

un ami
une amie

3 **Transformez** Change each word from the singular to the plural. Repeat the correct answer after the speaker. (*8 items*)

Modèle

un stylo
des stylos

4 **La classe** What does Sophie see in Professor Martin's French class? Listen to what she says and write the missing words in your lab manual.

1. _____ bureaux
2. _____ professeur
3. _____ étudiants en _____
4. des _____
5. le _____
6. les _____
7. _____ télévision
8. des _____

Unité 1 Lab Activities   **3**

Nom _____   Date _____

1A.2 Numbers 0–60

1 **Bingo** You are going to play two games (**jeux**) of bingo. As you hear each number, mark it with an **X** on your bingo card.

Jeu 1		
2	17	35
26	52	3
15	8	29
7	44	13

Jeu 2		
18	12	16
34	9	25
0	56	41
27	31	58

2 **Numéros** You want to know everything about your friend Marc's new university. Write down his answers to your questions.

> **Modèle**
> *You see:* professeurs de littérature
> *You say:* Il y a des professeurs de littérature?
> *You hear:* Oui, il y a dix-huit professeurs de littérature.
> *You write:* 18

1. étudiants américains _____
2. ordinateurs dans la bibliothèque _____
3. télévision dans la classe de littérature _____
4. bureaux dans la classe de sociologie _____
5. tables dans le café _____
6. tableaux dans le bureau du professeur de français _____

3 **Les maths** You will hear a series of math problems. Write the missing numbers and solve the problems.

> **Modèle**
> Combien font deux plus trois?
> 2 + 3 = 5

plus = *plus*   **moins** = *minus*   **font** = *equals (makes)*

1. ___ + ___ = ___   5. ___ − ___ = ___
2. ___ − ___ = ___   6. ___ + ___ = ___
3. ___ + ___ = ___   7. ___ + ___ = ___
4. ___ − ___ = ___   8. ___ − ___ = ___

4 **Questions** Look at the drawing and answer each question you hear. Repeat the correct response after the speaker. (*5 items*)

Unité 1
ESPACE CONTEXTES

Leçon 1B

1 Identifiez Look at the drawing and listen to the statement. Indicate whether each statement is **vrai** or **faux**.

	Vrai	Faux
1.	○	○
2.	○	○
3.	○	○
4.	○	○
5.	○	○
6.	○	○
7.	○	○
8.	○	○

2 Les contraires You will hear a list of masculine nouns. Write the number of the masculine noun next to its feminine counterpart.

_____ a. la femme

_____ b. une élève

_____ c. une camarade de classe

_____ d. la fille

_____ e. une étudiante

_____ f. madame

_____ g. l'actrice

_____ h. une copine

3 Professeur This professor needs to order new items at the bookstore. You will hear a series of questions. Look at the professor's list and answer each question. Then repeat the correct response after the speaker.

Liste

- 49 crayons
- 55 stylos
- 35 cahiers
- 31 livres
- 12 dictionnaires
- 18 cartes
- 5 corbeilles à papier
- 54 feuilles

LES SONS ET LES LETTRES

Silent letters

Final consonants of French words are usually silent.

    françai~~s~~   spor~~t~~   vou~~s~~   salu~~t~~

An unaccented -e (or -es) at the end of a word is silent, but the preceding consonant
is pronounced.

    français~~e~~   américain~~e~~   orang~~es~~   japonais~~es~~

The consonants -c, -r, -f, and -l are usually pronounced at the ends of words. To remember these
exceptions, think of the consonants in the word careful.

par**c**	bonjou**r**	acti**f**	anima**l**
la**c**	professeu**r**	naï**f**	ma**l**

---

1   **Prononcez** Practice saying these words aloud.

1. traditionnel	6. Monsieur	11. timide
2. étudiante	7. journalistes	12. sénégalais
3. généreuse	8. hôtel	13. objet
4. téléphones	9. sac	14. normal
5. chocolat	10. concert	15. importante

---

2   **Articulez** Practice saying these sentences aloud.

1. Au revoir, Paul. À plus tard!
2. Je vais très bien. Et vous, Monsieur Dubois?
3. Qu'est-ce que c'est? C'est une calculatrice.
4. Il y a un ordinateur, une table et une chaise.
5. Frédéric et Chantal, je vous présente Michel et Éric.
6. Voici un sac à dos, des crayons et des feuilles de papier.

---

3   **Dictons** Practice reading these sayings aloud.

1. Mieux vaut tard que jamais.
2. Aussitôt dit, aussitôt fait.

---

4   **Dictée** You will hear a conversation. Listen carefully and write what you hear during the pauses.
The entire conversation will then be repeated so you can check your work.

AMÉLIE _____

NICOLAS _____

AMÉLIE _____

NICOLAS _____

AMÉLIE _____

NICOLAS _____

AMÉLIE _____

ESPACE STRUCTURES

1B.1 The verb être

1 **Identifiez** For each drawing, you will hear two statements. Choose the one that corresponds to the drawing.

 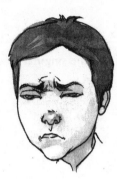  

1. a.   b.   2. a.   b.   3. a.   b.   4. a.   b.

2 **Complétez** Listen to the following sentences and write the missing verb. Repeat the sentence.

1. Je _____ étudiante à Boston.

2. Mon amie Maéva _____ suisse.

3. Nous _____ des États-Unis.

4. Mes professeurs _____ intéressants.

5. Vous _____ Madame Dufour?

6. Tu _____ en retard.

3 **Questions** Answer each question you hear. Repeat the correct response after the speaker.

> **Modèle**
> *You hear:* Et toi?
> *You see:* timide
> *You say:* Je suis timide.

1. égoïste
2. intelligent
3. sincère
4. difficile
5. brillant

1B.2 Adjective agreement

1 **Masculin ou féminin?** Change each sentence from the masculine to the feminine or vice versa. Repeat the correct answer after the speaker. (*6 items*)

> **Modèle**
> L'homme est français.
> *La femme est française.*

2 **Singulier ou pluriel?** Change each sentence from the singular to the plural and vice versa. Repeat the correct answer after the speaker. (*6 items*)

> **Modèle**
> Le garçon est sympathique.
> *Les garçons sont sympathiques.*

3 **Mes camarades de classe.** Describe your classmates using the cues in your lab manual. Repeat the correct response after the speaker.

> **Modèle**
> *You hear:* Anissa
> *You see:* amusant
> *You say:* Anissa est amusante.

1. intelligent   5. élégant
2. patient   6. sociable
3. égoïste   7. poli
4. optimiste   8. différent

4 **Complétez** Listen to the following description and write the missing words in your lab manual.

Brigitte (1) _____ (2) _____. Elle et Paul, un

(3) _____, (4) _____ étudiants à (5) _____

de Laval. Ils (6) _____ (7) _____. Paul est étudiant

en (8) _____ et Brigitte, en (9) _____

(10) _____. Dans le cours de français, il y a des (11) _____

et des (12) _____; il y a aussi une (13) _____ et une

(14) _____. Les étudiants sont très (15) _____,

(16) _____ et (17) _____.

Unité 2

ESPACE CONTEXTES

1 **Classifiez** Indicate whether each word you hear is a person (**personne**), a course (**cours**), an object (**objet**), or a place (**endroit**).

	personne	cours	objet	endroit
1.	_____	_____	_____	_____
2.	_____	_____	_____	_____
3.	_____	_____	_____	_____
4.	_____	_____	_____	_____
5.	_____	_____	_____	_____
6.	_____	_____	_____	_____
7.	_____	_____	_____	_____
8.	_____	_____	_____	_____

2 **Décrivez** For each drawing you will hear two statements. Choose the one that corresponds to the drawing.

1. a.   b.   2. a.   b.   3. a.   b.   4. a.   b.

3 **Les cours** You will hear six people talking about their favorite topics. Decide which classes they attend.

1. _____   a. chimie
2. _____   b. psychologie
3. _____   c. philosophie
4. _____   d. géographie
5. _____   e. stylisme
6. _____   f. histoire

LES SONS ET LES LETTRES

Liaisons

Consonants at the end of French words are generally silent, but are usually pronounced when the word that follows begins with a vowel sound. This linking of sounds is called a liaison.

À tout à l'heure!   Comment allez-vous?

An **s** or an **x** in a liaison sounds like the letter *z*.

les étudiants   trois élèves   six élèves   deux hommes

Always make a liaison between a subject pronoun and a verb that begins with a vowel sound; always make a liaison between an article and a noun that begins with a vowel sound.

nous aimons   ils ont   un étudiant   les ordinateurs

Always make a liaison between **est** (a form of **être**) and a word that begins with a vowel or a vowel sound. Never make a liaison with the final consonant of a proper name.

Robert est anglais.   Paris est exceptionnelle.

Never make a liaison with the conjunction **et** (*and*).

Carole et Hélène   Jacques et Antoinette

Never make a liaison between a singular noun and an adjective that follows it.

un cours horrible   un instrument élégant

1 **Prononcez** Practice saying these words and expressions aloud.

1. un examen
2. des étudiants
3. les hôtels
4. dix acteurs
5. Paul et Yvette
6. cours important
7. des informations
8. les études
9. deux hommes
10. Bernard aime
11. chocolat italien
12. Louis est

2 **Articulez** Practice saying these sentences aloud.

1. Nous aimons les arts.
2. Albert habite à Paris.
3. C'est un objet intéressant.
4. Sylvie est avec Anne.
5. Ils adorent les deux universités.

3 **Dictons** Practice reading these sayings aloud.

1. Les amis de nos amis sont nos amis.
2. Un hôte non invité doit apporter son siège.

4 **Dictée** You will hear a conversation. Listen carefully and write what you hear during the pauses. The entire conversation will then be repeated so you can check your work.

ANNE _____

PATRICK _____

ANNE _____

PATRICK _____

ANNE _____

PATRICK _____

ESPACE STRUCTURES

2A.1 Present tense of regular -er verbs

1 **À l'université** Describe your activities at the university using the cues in your lab manual. Repeat the correct response after the speaker.

> **Modèle**
>
> _You hear:_ Édouard
> _You see:_ manger au resto U
> _You say:_ Édouard mange au resto U.

1. adorer la mode
2. détester les examens
3. étudier à la bibliothèque
4. retrouver des amis au café
5. aimer mieux la philosophie
6. penser que la chimie est difficile

2 **Changez** Listen to the following statements. Using the cues you hear, say that these people do the same activities. Repeat the correct answer after the speaker. (_8 items_)

> **Modèle**
>
> J'étudie l'architecture. (Charles)
> _Charles étudie l'architecture._

3 **Choisissez** Listen to each statement and choose the most logical response.

1. a. Nous mangeons.   b. Vous mangez.
2. a. Vous travaillez.   b. Ils travaillent.
3. a. Nous regardons la télé.   b. Nous dessinons la télé.
4. a. Tu habites à Paris.   b. J'habite à Paris.
5. a. Elle aime travailler ici.   b. Elles aiment travailler ici.
6. a. Tu adores parler.   b. Tu détestes parler.

4 **Regardez** Listen to each statement and write the number of the statement below the drawing it describes.

a. _____   b. _____   c. _____   d. _____

2A.2 Forming questions and expressing negation

1 **Mes camarades de classe** You want to know about your classmates, so you ask your friend Simon questions with **est-ce que** using the cues in your lab manual. Repeat the correct question after the speaker.

> *Modèle*
>
> *You hear:* parler en cours
> *You see:* Bertrand
> *You say:* Est-ce que Bertrand parle en cours?

1. Émilie
2. toi
3. Antoine et Ahmed
4. Pierre-Étienne
5. Sophie et toi
6. Sara et Maude

2 **Questions** You want to know about your classmates, so you ask your friend Guillaume questions with inversion using the cues in your lab manual. Repeat the correct question after the speaker.

> *Modèle*
>
> *You hear:* chercher un livre
> *You see:* Catherine
> *You say:* Catherine cherche-t-elle un livre?

1. toi
2. Marie
3. Michel et toi
4. Martin
5. le professeur
6. vous

3 **Répondez** Answer each question in the negative. Repeat the correct response after the speaker. (*6 items*)

> *Modèle*
>
> Est-ce que tu habites en France?
> Non, je n'habite pas en France.

4 **Complétez** Listen to the conversation between Mathilde and David. Answer the questions in your lab manual.

1. Est-ce que Mathilde aime les maths?

   _____

2. Pourquoi est-ce qu'elle déteste la biologie?

   _____

3. Est-ce qu'il y a des étudiants sympas?

   _____

4. Est-ce que le professeur de physique est ennuyeux?

   _____

5. Y a-t-il des étudiants stupides dans la classe de David?

   _____

Unité 2

ESPACE CONTEXTES

Leçon 2B

1 **L'emploi du temps** You will hear a series of statements. Look at Élisabeth's schedule and indicate whether the statements are **vrai** or **faux**.

	lundi	mardi	mercredi	jeudi	vendredi	samedi	dimanche
matin	cours de français		téléphoner à Florence		cours de français		
après-midi		examen de maths		cours de danse		visiter Tours avec Carole	
soir	préparer examen de maths		dîner avec Christian			dîner en famille	dîner en famille

	Vrai	Faux			Vrai	Faux
1.	○	○		5.	○	○
2.	○	○		6.	○	○
3.	○	○		7.	○	○
4.	○	○		8.	○	○

2 **Quel jour?** Olivier is never sure what day of the week it is. Respond to his questions saying that it is the day before the one he mentions. Then repeat the correct answer after the speaker. (6 *items*)

> **Modèle**
>
> Aujourd'hui, c'est mercredi, n'est-ce pas?
> Non, aujourd'hui, *c'est mardi.*

3 **Complétez** Listen to this description and write the missing words in your lab manual.

Je (1) _____ Nathalie et j' (2) _____ en Californie.

J' (3) _____ le français et j' (4) _____ la grammaire à

l'Alliance française. Les étudiants (5) _____ un peu. Ils

(6) _____ des vidéos et ils (7) _____ des CD. Ils

(8) _____ beaucoup mais ils (9) _____ la classe amusante.

Après le cours, les étudiants et moi, nous (10) _____ dans un restaurant français.

LES SONS ET LES LETTRES

The letter r

The French **r** is very different from the English *r*. The English *r* is pronounced by placing the tongue in the middle and toward the front of the mouth. The French **r** is pronounced in the throat.

You have seen that an **-er** at the end of a word is usually pronounced **-ay**, as in the English word *way*, but without the glide sound.

chant**er**   mang**er**   expliqu**er**   aim**er**

In most other cases, the French **r** has a very different sound. Pronunciation of the French **r** varies according to its position in a word. Note the different ways the **r** is pronounced in these words.

rivière   littérature   ordinateur   devoir

If an **r** falls between two vowels or before a vowel, it is pronounced with slightly more friction.

rare   garage   Europe   rose

An **r** sound before a consonant or at the end of a word is pronounced with slightly less friction.

porte   bourse   adore   jour

1 **Prononcez** Practice saying the following words aloud.

1. crayon	5. terrible	9. rentrer	13. être
2. professeur	6. architecture	10. regarder	14. dernière
3. plaisir	7. trouver	11. lettres	15. arriver
4. différent	8. restaurant	12. réservé	16. après

2 **Articulez** Practice saying the following sentences aloud.

1. Au revoir, Professeur Colbert!
2. Rose arrive en retard mardi.
3. Mercredi, c'est le dernier jour des cours.
4. Robert et Roger adorent écouter la radio.
5. La corbeille à papier, c'est quarante-quatre euros!
6. Les parents de Richard sont brillants et très agréables.

3 **Dictons** Practice reading these sayings aloud.

1. Qui ne risque rien n'a rien.
2. Quand le renard prêche, gare aux oies.

4 **Dictée** You will hear six sentences. Each will be read twice. Listen carefully and write what you hear.

1. _____

2. _____

3. _____

4. _____

5. _____

6. _____

ESPACE STRUCTURES

2B.1 Present tense of avoir

1 **Question d'opinion** People don't always do what they should. Say what they have to do. Repeat the correct answer after the speaker. (*6 items*)

> **Modèle**
> Lucie ne mange pas le matin.
> *Lucie a besoin de manger le matin.*

2 **Changez** Form a new sentence using the cue you hear. Repeat the correct answer after the speaker. (*6 items*)

> **Modèle**
> J'ai sommeil. (nous)
> *Nous avons sommeil.*

3 **Répondez** Answer each question you hear using the cues in your lab manual. Repeat the correct answer after the speaker.

> **Modèle**
> Tu as chaud? (non)
> *Non, je n'ai pas chaud.*

1. oui   3. non   5. non
2. non   4. oui   6. non

4 **Choisissez** Listen to each situation and choose the appropriate expression. Each situation will be read twice.

1. a. Elle a honte.   b. Elle a de la chance.
2. a. J'ai tort.   b. J'ai raison.
3. a. Il a peur.   b. Il a froid.
4. a. Nous avons chaud.   b. Nous avons sommeil.
5. a. Vous avez de la chance. b. Vous avez l'air gentil.
6. a. Ils ont envie.   b. Ils ont tort.

2B.2 Telling time

1 **L'heure** Look at the clock and listen to the statement. Indicate whether the statement is **vrai** or **faux**.

1. vrai ○   2. vrai ○   3. vrai ○   4. vrai ○   5. vrai ○   6. vrai ○
   faux ○   faux ○   faux ○   faux ○   faux ○   faux ○

2 **Quelle heure est-il?** Your friends want to know the time. Answer their questions using the cues in your lab manual. Repeat the correct response after the speaker.

> **Modèle**
> *You hear:* Quelle heure est-il?
> *You see:* 2:15 p.m.
> *You say:* Il est deux heures et quart de l'après-midi.

1. 10:25 a.m.   3. 7:45 p.m.   5. 9:15 a.m.   7. 5:20 p.m.
2. 12:10 a.m.   4. 3:30 p.m.   6. 10:50 p.m.   8. 12:30 p.m.

3 **À quelle heure?** You are trying to plan your class schedule. Ask your counselor what time these classes meet and write the answer.

> **Modèle**
> *You see:* le cours de géographie
> *You say:* À quelle heure est le cours de géographie?
> *You hear:* Il est à neuf heures et demie du matin.
> *You write:* 9:30 a.m.

1. le cours de biologie _____   4. le cours d'allemand _____
2. le cours d'informatique _____   5. le cours de chimie _____
3. le cours de maths _____   6. le cours de littérature _____

4 **Les trains** Your friend is in Paris and plans to go to the Riviera. He wants to know the train schedule. Using the 24-hour clock, answer his questions using the cues in your lab manual. Repeat the correct response after the speaker.

> **Modèle**
> *You hear:* À quelle heure est le dernier train pour Nice?
> *You see:* 7:30 p.m.
> *You say:* Il est à dix-neuf heures trente.

1. 9:05 p.m.   3. 10:30 a.m.   5. 12:23 p.m.
2. 8:15 a.m.   4. 5:25 p.m.   6. 10:27 p.m.

Unité 3

ESPACE CONTEXTES

Leçon 3A

1 **Qui est-ce?** You will hear some questions. Look at the family tree and give the correct answer to each question.

La famille Martin

Paul   Lucie

Gérard   Sophie   Édouard   Mathilde

Lise   Tristan   Antoine   Myriam   Jérôme

1. _____
2. _____
3. _____
4. _____
5. _____
6. _____
7. _____
8. _____
9. _____
10. _____

2 **La famille Martin** Lise's new friend just met her family and wants to verify the various relationships. Look at the family tree in **Activité 1,** and answer the questions. Repeat the answer after the speaker. (*6 items*)

> **Modèle**
> Paul est le frère de Gérard, n'est-ce pas?
> *Non, Paul est le beau-père de Gérard.*

3 **Complétez** Listen to this story and write the missing words in your lab manual.

Je m'appelle Julien. Mes (1) _____ sont divorcés. J'habite avec ma

(2) _____ et ma (3) _____. Nous partageons une maison avec le

(4) _____ de ma (5) _____. Mon (6) _____ et ma

(7) _____ ont trois (8) _____. Mon (9) _____ s'appelle

Simon et mes (10) _____ s'appellent Coralie et Sixtine. Mon

(11) _____ est marié et ma (12) _____ s'appelle Sabine. J'ai un

(13) _____ Théophile.

LES SONS ET LES LETTRES

L'accent aigu and l'accent grave

In French, diacritical marks (accents) are an essential part of a word's spelling. They indicate how vowels are pronounced or distinguish between words with similar spellings but different meanings. **L'accent aigu** (´) appears only over the vowel **e**. It indicates that the **e** is pronounced similarly to the vowel *a* in the English word *cake* but shorter and crisper.

étudier	réservé	élégant	téléphone

L'accent aigu also signals some similarities between French and English words. Often, an **e** with **l'accent aigu** at the beginning of a French word marks the place where the letter *s* would appear at the beginning of the English equivalent.

éponge	épouse	état	étudiante
sponge	*spouse*	*state*	*student*

L'accent grave (`) appears only over the vowels **a**, **e**, and **u**. Over the vowel **e**, it indicates that the **e** is pronounced like the vowel *e* in the English word *pet*.

très	après	mère	nièce

Although **l'accent grave** does not change the pronunciation of the vowels *a* or *u*, it distinguishes words that have a similar spelling but different meanings.

la	là	ou	où
the	*there*	*or*	*where*

1 **Prononcez** Practice saying these words aloud.

1. agréable	3. voilà	5. frère	7. déjà	9. lycée	11. là
2. sincère	4. faculté	6. à	8. éléphant	10. poème	12. élève

2 **Articulez** Practice saying these sentences aloud.

1. À tout à l'heure!
2. Thérèse, je te présente Michèle.
3. Hélène est très sérieuse et réservée.
4. Voilà mon père, Frédéric, et ma mère, Ségolène.
5. Tu préfères étudier à la fac demain après-midi?

3 **Dictons** Practice saying these sayings aloud.

1. Tel père, tel fils.
2. À vieille mule, frein doré.

4 **Dictée** You will hear eight sentences. Each will be said twice. Listen carefully and write what you hear.

1. _____
2. _____
3. _____
4. _____
5. _____
6. _____
7. _____
8. _____

ESPACE STRUCTURES

3A.1 Descriptive adjectives

1 **Féminin ou masculin?** Change each sentence from the masculine to the feminine or vice versa. Repeat the correct answer after the speaker. (6 *items*)

> **Modèle**
>
> L'oncle de Marie est français.
> La tante de Marie est française.

2 **Singulier ou pluriel?** Change each sentence from singular to plural and vice versa. Repeat the correct answer after the speaker. (6 *items*)

> **Modèle**
>
> L'élève est jeune.
> Les élèves sont jeunes.

3 **Mes camarades de classe** Describe your classmates using the cues in your lab manual. Repeat the correct answer after the speaker.

> **Modèle**
>
> *You hear:* Jeanne
> *You see:* petit
> *You say:* Jeanne est petite.

1. brun
2. roux
3. beau
4. sympathique
5. grand et gros
6. heureux et intelligent
7. bon et naïf
8. nouveau

4 **La famille Dumoulin** Look at the picture of the Dumoulin family. Listen to these statements and decide whether each statement is **vrai** or **faux**.

	Vrai	Faux
1.	○	○
2.	○	○
3.	○	○
4.	○	○
5.	○	○
6.	○	○
7.	○	○
8.	○	○

3A.2 Possessive adjectives

1 **Identifiez** Listen to each statement and mark an **X** in the column for the correct translation of the possessive adjective you hear.

> **Modèle**
> You hear: C'est mon professeur de français.
> You mark: an **X** under my

	my	your (familiar)	your (formal)	his/her	our	their
Modèle	X					
1.						
2.						
3.						
4.						
5.						
6.						
7.						
8.						

2 **Choisissez** Listen to each question and choose the most logical answer.

1. a. Oui, ton appartement est grand.
   b. Non, mon appartement n'est pas grand.
2. a. Oui, nous habitons avec nos parents.
   b. Non, nous n'habitons pas avec vos parents.
3. a. Oui, c'est ton cousin.
   b. Oui, c'est son cousin.
4. a. Oui, leurs parents rentrent à 10 heures ce soir.
   b. Oui, nos parents rentrent à 10 heures ce soir.
5. a. Non, ma sœur n'étudie pas la chimie.
   b. Non, sa sœur n'étudie pas la chimie.
6. a. Oui, leur nièce est au Brésil.
   b. Oui, ma nièce est au Brésil.
7. a. Non, leurs amis ne sont pas ici.
   b. Non, nos amis ne sont pas ici.
8. a. Oui, leurs grands-parents sont italiens.
   b. Oui, nos grands-parents sont italiens.

3 **Questions** Answer each question you hear in the affirmative using the appropriate possessive adjective. Repeat the correct response after the speaker. (*6 items*)

> **Modèle**
> C'est ton ami?
> Oui, c'est mon ami.

Unité 3

ESPACE CONTEXTES

Leçon 3B

---

1 **Logique ou illogique?** Listen to these statements and indicate whether they are **logique** or **illogique**.

	Logique	Illogique			Logique	Illogique
1.	○	○		5.	○	○
2.	○	○		6.	○	○
3.	○	○		7.	○	○
4.	○	○		8.	○	○

2 **Associez** Circle the words that are logically associated with each word you hear.

1. actif   sportif   faible
2. drôle   pénible   antipathique
3. cruel   mauvais   gentil
4. modeste   intelligent   prêt
5. favori   lent   homme d'affaires
6. architecte   fou   ennuyeux

3 **Professions** Listen to each statement and write the number of the statement below the photo it describes. There are more statements than there are photos.

a. _____   b. _____   c. _____

d. _____   e. _____

LES SONS ET LES LETTRES

L'accent circonflexe, la cédille, and le tréma

L'accent circonflexe (ˆ) can appear over any vowel.

pâté	prêt	aîné	drôle	croûton

L'accent circonflexe is also used to distinguish between words with similar spellings but different meanings.

mûr	**mur**	**sûr**	**sur**
ripe	*wall*	*sure*	*on*

L'accent circonflexe indicates that a letter, frequently an *s*, has been dropped from an older spelling. For this reason, l'accent circonflexe can be used to identify French cognates of English words.

hospital → hôpital   forest → forêt

La cédille (¸) is only used with the letter c. A c with a cédille is pronounced with a soft c sound, like the *s* in the English word *yes*. Use a cédille to retain the soft c sound before an a, o, or u. Before an e or an i, the letter c is always soft, so a cédille is not necessary.

garçon	français	ça	leçon

Le tréma (¨) is used to indicate that two vowel sounds are pronounced separately. It is always placed over the second vowel.

égoïste	naïve	Noël	Haïti

---

1 **Prononcez** Practice saying these words aloud.

1. naïf	3. châtain	5. français	7. théâtre	9. égoïste
2. reçu	4. âge	6. fenêtre	8. garçon	10. château

---

2 **Articulez** Practice saying these sentences aloud.

1. Comment ça va?
2. Comme ci, comme ça.
3. Vous êtes française, Madame?
4. C'est un garçon cruel et égoïste.
5. J'ai besoin d'être reçu(e) à l'examen.
6. Caroline, ma sœur aînée, est très drôle.

---

3 **Dictons** Practice reading these sayings aloud.

1. Impossible n'est pas français.
2. Plus ça change, plus c'est la même chose.

---

4 **Dictée** You will hear six sentences. Each will be read twice. Listen carefully and write what you hear.

1. _____
2. _____
3. _____
4. _____
5. _____
6. _____

ESPACE STRUCTURES

3B.1 Numbers 61–100

1 **Numéros de téléphone** You are at a party and you meet some new people. You want to see them again but you don't have their telephone numbers. Ask them what their phone numbers are and write their answers.

> **Modèle**
>
> _You see:_ Julie
> _You say:_ Quel est ton numéro de téléphone, Julie?
> _You hear:_ C'est le zéro un, vingt-trois, trente-huit,
> quarante-trois, cinquante-deux.
> _You write:_ 01.23.38.43.52

1. Chloé _____
2. Justin _____
3. Ibrahim _____
4. Cassandre _____
5. Lolita _____
6. Yannis _____
7. Omar _____
8. Sara _____

2 **Inventaire** You and your co-worker are taking an inventory at the university bookstore. Answer your co-worker's questions using the cue in your lab manual. Repeat the correct response after the speaker.

> **Modèle**
>
> _You hear:_ Il y a combien de livres de français?
> _You see:_ 61
> _You say:_ Il y a soixante et un livres de français.

1. 71   3. 87   5. 62   7. 83
2. 92   4. 94   6. 96   8. 66

3 **Message** Listen to this telephone conversation and complete the phone message in your lab manual with the correct information.

MESSAGE TÉLÉPHONIQUE
Pour: _____
De: _____
Téléphone: _____
Message: _____
_____

3B.2 Prepositions of location

1 **Décrivez** Look at the drawing and listen to each statement. Indicate whether each statement is vrai or faux.

	Vrai	Faux
1.	○	○
2.	○	○
3.	○	○
4.	○	○
5.	○	○
6.	○	○
7.	○	○
8.	○	○

2 **Où est...?** Using the drawing from **Activité 1** and the cues in your lab manual, say where these items are located. Repeat the correct response after the speaker.

> **Modèle**
>
> *You see:* entre
> *You hear:* le cahier
> *You say:* Le cahier est entre les crayons et les livres.

1. à côté de   3. en face de   5. devant   7. derrière
2. à droite de   4. près de   6. sur   8. à gauche de

3 **Complétez** Listen to the conversation and correct these statements.

1. Francine habite chez ses parents.

_____

2. La résidence est près des salles de classe.

_____

3. Le gymnase est loin de la résidence.

_____

4. La bibliothèque est derrière le café.

_____

5. Le cinéma est en face du café.

_____

6. Le resto U est derrière la bibliothèque.

_____

Unité 4

ESPACE CONTEXTES

---

1 **Choisissez** Listen to each question and choose the most logical answer.

1. a. Non, je ne nage pas.
   b. Oui, elle mange à la piscine.
2. a. Oui, j'ai très faim.
   b. Non, il mange au restaurant.
3. a. Non, elle est au bureau.
   b. Oui, elle adore aller au centre commercial.
4. a. Non, il est absent.
   b. Non, ils sont absents.
5. a. Oui, ils ont une maison en banlieue.
   b. Non, ils sont au musée.
6. a. Oui, elle va à la montagne.
   b. Oui, elle danse beaucoup.
7. a. Oui, on va passer.
   b. Non, nous ne sommes pas chez nous ici.
8. a. Non, je n'aime pas aller en ville.
   b. Non, ils sont trop jeunes.

---

2 **Les lieux** You will hear six people describe what they are doing. Choose the place that corresponds to the activity.

1. _____   a. au café
2. _____   b. au musée
3. _____   c. au centre commercial
4. _____   d. à la bibliothèque
5. _____   e. au gymnase
6. _____   f. au restaurant

---

3 **Décrivez** You will hear two statements for each drawing. Choose the one that corresponds to the drawing.

  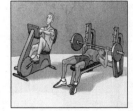 

1. a.   b.   2. a.   b.   3. a.   b.   4. a.   b.

LES SONS ET LES LETTRES

Oral vowels

French has two basic kinds of vowel sounds: oral vowels, the subject of this discussion, and nasal vowels, presented in **Leçon 4B**. Oral vowels are produced by releasing air through the mouth. The pronunciation of French vowels is consistent and predictable.

In short words (usually two-letter words), **e** is pronounced similarly to the *a* in the English word *about*.

    le   que   ce   de

The letter **a** alone is pronounced like the a in *father*.

    la   ça   ma   ta

The letter **i** by itself and the letter **y** are pronounced like the vowel sound in the word *bee*.

    ici   livre   stylo   lycée

The letter combination **ou** sounds like the vowel sound in the English word *who*.

    vous   nous   **ou**blier   écouter

The French **u** sound does not exist in English. To produce this sound, say *ee* with your lips rounded.

    tu   du   une   étudier

1   **Prononcez** Répétez les mots suivants à voix haute.

1. je	5. utile	9. mari	13. gymnase
2. chat	6. place	10. active	14. antipathique
3. fou	7. jour	11. Sylvie	15. calculatrice
4. ville	8. triste	12. rapide	16. piscine

2   **Articulez** Répétez les phrases suivantes à voix haute.

1. Salut, Luc. Ça va?
2. La philosophie est difficile.
3. Brigitte est une actrice fantastique.
4. Suzanne va à son cours de physique.
5. Tu trouves le cours de maths facile?
6. Viviane a une bourse universitaire.

3   **Dictons** Répétez les dictons à voix haute.

1. Qui va à la chasse perd sa place.   2. Plus on est de fous, plus on rit.

4   **Dictée** You will hear eight sentences. Each will be read twice. Listen carefully and write what you hear.

1. _____
2. _____
3. _____
4. _____
5. _____
6. _____
7. _____
8. _____

ESPACE STRUCTURES

4A.1 The verb aller

1 Identifiez Listen to each statement and mark an **X** in the column of the subject of the verb you hear.

> **Modèle**
> *You hear:* Il ne va pas au cours de mathématiques aujourd'hui.
> *You mark:* an **X** under **il**

	je	tu	il/elle/on	nous	vous	ils/elles
Modèle			X			
1.						
2.						
3.						
4.						
5.						
6.						
7.						
8.						

2 Où vont-ils? Describe where these people are going using the cue in your lab manual. Repeat the correct answer after the speaker.

> **Modèle**
> *You hear:* Samuel
> *You see:* marché
> *You say:* Samuel va au marché.

1. épicerie
2. parc
3. magasin
4. église
5. hôpital
6. café
7. montagne
8. centre-ville

3 Transformez Change each sentence from the present to the immediate future. Repeat the correct answer after the speaker. (*6 items*)

> **Modèle**
> Régine bavarde avec sa voisine.
> *Régine va bavarder avec sa voisine.*

4 Présent ou futur? Listen to each statement and indicate if the sentence is in the present or the immediate future.

	Présent	Futur proche			Présent	Futur proche
1.	○	○		5.	○	○
2.	○	○		6.	○	○
3.	○	○		7.	○	○
4.	○	○		8.	○	○

4A.2 Interrogative words

1 **Logique ou illogique?** You will hear some questions and responses. Decide if they are **logique** or **illogique**.

	Logique	Illogique			Logique	Illogique
1.	O	O		5.	O	O
2.	O	O		6.	O	O
3.	O	O		7.	O	O
4.	O	O		8.	O	O

2 **Questions** Answer each question you hear using the cue in your lab manual. Repeat the correct answer after the speaker. (*6 items*)

> **Modèle**
> *You hear:* Pourquoi est-ce que
>   tu ne vas pas au café?
> *You see:* aller travailler
> *You say:* Parce que je vais travailler.

1. chez lui
2. avec sa cousine
3. Bertrand
4. à un journaliste
5. absent
6. sérieux

3 **Questions** Listen to each answer and ask the question that prompted the answer. Repeat the correct question after the speaker. (*6 items*)

> **Modèle**
> *You hear:* Grégoire va au bureau.
> *You say:* Où va Grégoire?

4 **Conversation** Listen to the conversation and answer the questions.

1. Pourquoi est-ce que Pauline aime son nouvel appartement?

   _____

2. Où est cet appartement?

   _____

3. Comment est la propriétaire?

   _____

4. Combien de personnes travaillent au musée?

   _____

Unité 4

ESPACE CONTEXTES

Leçon 4B

1 **Associez** Circle the words that are logically associated with each word you hear.

1. frites   baguette   limonade
2. table   sandwich   pourboire
3. beurre   addition   serveur
4. morceau   coûter   soif
5. verre   tasse   sucre
6. plusieurs   soupe   apporter

2 **Logique ou illogique?** Listen to these statements and indicate whether they are **logique** or **illogique**.

	Logique	Illogique			Logique	Illogique
1.	O	O		5.	O	O
2.	O	O		6.	O	O
3.	O	O		7.	O	O
4.	O	O		8.	O	O

3 **Décrivez** Listen to each sentence and write the number of the sentence on the line pointing to the food or drink mentioned.

a. _____

b. _____

c. _____

d. _____

4 **Complétez** Listen to this story and write the missing words in your lab manual.

Bonjour, je m'appelle Raymond. J'aime les journées (1) _____ *La Rotonde*, près

de chez moi. Le matin, je commence un livre avec un bon café au (2) _____.

Le midi, j'adore être à la terrasse. Je mange un sandwich (3) _____ ou jambon

(4) _____. Quand j'ai froid, j'aime mieux (5) _____.

L'après-midi, je (6) _____ avec les (7) _____. Ils sont

sympas, alors je laisse toujours un bon (8) _____.

LES SONS ET LES LETTRES

Nasal vowels

When vowels are followed by an **m** or an **n** in a single syllable, they usually become nasal vowels. Nasal vowels are produced by pushing air through both the mouth and the nose.

The nasal vowel sound you hear in **français** is usually spelled **an** or **en**.

    an   fr**an**çais   **en**chanté   **enf**ant

The nasal vowel sound you hear in **bien** may be spelled **en**, **in**, **im**, **ain**, or **aim**. The nasal vowel sound you hear in **brun** may be spelled **un** or **um**.

    exam**en**   améric**ain**   l**un**di   parf**um**

The nasal vowel sound you hear in **bon** is spelled **on** or **om**.

    t**on**   all**ons**   c**om**bien   **on**cle

When **m** or **n** is followed by a vowel sound, the preceding vowel is not nasal.

    image   inutile   ami   amour

---

1 **Prononcez** Répétez les mots suivants à voix haute.

    1. blond   5. garçon   9. quelqu'un   13. impatient
    2. dans   6. avant   10. différent   14. rencontrer
    3. faim   7. maison   11. amusant   15. informatique
    4. entre   8. cinéma   12. télévision   16. comment

---

2 **Articulez** Répétez les phrases suivantes à voix haute.

    1. Mes parents ont cinquante ans.
    2. Tu prends une limonade, Martin?
    3. Le Printemps est un grand magasin.
    4. Lucien va prendre le train à Montauban.
    5. Pardon, Monsieur, l'addition s'il vous plaît!
    6. Jean-François a les cheveux bruns et les yeux marron.

---

3 **Dictons** Répétez les dictons à voix haute.

    1. L'appétit vient en mangeant.
    2. N'allonge pas ton bras au-delà de ta manche.

---

4 **Dictée** You will hear eight sentences. Each will be read twice. Listen carefully and write what you hear.

    1. _____
    2. _____
    3. _____
    4. _____
    5. _____
    6. _____
    7. _____
    8. _____

ESPACE STRUCTURES

4B.1 The verbs **prendre** and **boire**; Partitives

1 **Identifiez** Listen to each statement and mark an **X** in the column of the verb you hear.

> **Modèle**
> *You hear:* Nous n'allons pas apprendre
> le chinois cette année.
> *You mark:* an **X** under **apprendre**

	apprendre	prendre	comprendre	boire
Modèle	X			
1.				
2.				
3.				
4.				
5.				
6.				
7.				
8.				

2 **Décrivez** You will hear two statements for each drawing. Choose the one that corresponds to the drawing.

1. a.   b.   2. a.   b.   3. a.   b.   4. a.   b.

3 **Choisissez** Listen to each question and choose the most logical answer.

1. a. Non, elle n'a pas faim.
   b. Non, elle n'a pas soif.
2. a. Parce qu'il n'a pas de jambon.
   b. Parce que je prends aussi un chocolat.
3. a. Je ne prends pas de sucre.
   b. Oui, avec du sucre et un peu de lait.
4. a. Non, je n'aime pas le pain.
   b. Non, je prends du pain.

5. a. Oui, ils prennent ça tous les jours.
   b. Non, ils n'aiment pas le café.
6. a. Je bois un café.
   b. Je prends un éclair au café.
7. a. Quand elles ont soif.
   b. Non, elles n'ont pas soif.
8. a. Pourquoi pas.
   b. Oui, tout de suite.

4B.2 Regular -ir verbs

1 **Changez** Form a new sentence using the cue you hear as the subject. Repeat the correct answer after the speaker. (*8 items*)

> **Modèle**
> Je finis tous les devoirs de français. (nous)
> **Nous finissons tous les devoirs de français.**

2 **Répondez** Answer each question you hear using the cue in your lab manual. Repeat the correct response after the speaker.

> **Modèle**
> *You hear:* Qui choisit le gâteau au chocolat?
> *You see:* mes parents
> *You say:* **Mes parents choisissent le gâteau au chocolat.**

1. dix heures	3. il fait chaud	5. Béatrice et Julie
2. non	4. oui	6. oui

3 **Logique ou illogique?** Listen to each statement and indicate if it is **logique** or **illogique**.

	Logique	Illogique		Logique	Illogique
1.	O	O	5.	O	O
2.	O	O	6.	O	O
3.	O	O	7.	O	O
4.	O	O	8.	O	O

4 **Conversation** Listen to Antoine and Léa's conversation and answer the questions.

1. Pourquoi est-ce que Léa est heureuse? _____

2. Est-ce qu'elle a réussi ses examens? _____

3. Quel restaurant choisissent-ils? _____

4. Que prend Antoine à manger? _____

5. Antoine a-t-il peur de grossir? _____

6. Pourquoi Léa choisit-elle de prendre une salade? _____

Unité 5

ESPACE CONTEXTES

---

1   **Identifiez** You will hear a series of words. Write the word that does not belong in each series.

1. _____   5. _____

2. _____   6. _____

3. _____   7. _____

4. _____   8. _____

---

2   **Choisissez** Listen to each question and choose the most logical answer.

1. a. Oui, le lundi et le vendredi.
   b. Non, je déteste les bandes dessinées.
2. a. Chez mes parents.
   b. Rarement.
3. a. Avec mon ami.
   b. Une fois par mois.
4. a. Nous jouons pour gagner.
   b. Nous jouons surtout le soir.
5. a. Oui, j'aime le cinéma.
   b. J'aime mieux le golf.
6. a. Non, ils ne travaillent pas.
   b. Ils bricolent beaucoup.
7. a. Oui, son équipe est numéro un.
   b. Oui, c'est son passe-temps préféré.
8. a. Oui, ils jouent aujourd'hui.
   b. Il n'y a pas de spectacle.

---

3   **Les lieux** You will hear a couple describing their leisure activities on a typical weekend day. Write each activity in the appropriate space.

	la femme	l'homme
le matin	_____	_____
à midi	_____	_____
l'après-midi	_____	_____
le soir	_____	_____

LES SONS ET LES LETTRES

Intonation

In short, declarative sentences, the pitch of your voice, or intonation, falls on the final word or syllable.

Nathalie est française.   **Hector joue au football.**

In longer, declarative sentences, intonation rises, then falls.

À trois heures et demie, j'ai sciences politiques.

In sentences containing lists, intonation rises for each item in the list and falls on the last syllable of the last one.

Martine est jeune, blonde et jolie.

In long, declarative sentences, such as those containing clauses, intonation may rise several times, falling on the final syllable.

Le samedi, à dix heures du matin, je vais au centre commercial.

Questions that require a yes or no answer have rising intonation. Information questions have falling intonation.

C'est ta mère?   **Est-ce qu'elle joue au tennis?**

Quelle heure est-il?   **Quand est-ce que tu arrives?**

---

1   **Prononcez** Répétez les phrases suivantes à voix haute.

1. J'ai dix-neuf ans.
2. Tu fais du sport?
3. Quel jour sommes-nous?
4. Sandrine n'habite pas à Paris.
5. Quand est-ce que Marc arrive?
6. Charlotte est sérieuse et intellectuelle.

---

2   **Articulez** Répétez les dialogues à voix haute.

1. —Qu'est-ce que c'est?
   —C'est un ordinateur.
2. —Tu es américaine?
   —Non, je suis canadienne.
3. —Qu'est-ce que Christine étudie?
   —Elle étudie l'anglais et l'espagnol.
4. —Où est le musée?
   —Il est en face de l'église.

---

3   **Dictons** Répétez les dictons à voix haute.

1. Si le renard court, le poulet a des ailes.
2. Petit à petit, l'oiseau fait son nid.

---

4   **Dictée** You will hear eight sentences. Each will be read twice. Listen carefully and write what you hear.

1. _____
2. _____
3. _____
4. _____
5. _____
6. _____
7. _____
8. _____

ESPACE STRUCTURES

5A.1 The verb faire

1   **Identifiez**   Listen to each statement and mark an **X** in the column of the verb form you hear.

> **Modèle**
>
> *You hear:* François ne fait pas de sport.
> *You mark:* an **X** under **fait**

	fais	fait	faisons	faites	font
Modèle	_____	X	_____	_____	_____
1.	_____	_____	_____	_____	_____
2.	_____	_____	_____	_____	_____
3.	_____	_____	_____	_____	_____
4.	_____	_____	_____	_____	_____
5.	_____	_____	_____	_____	_____
6.	_____	_____	_____	_____	_____
7.	_____	_____	_____	_____	_____
8.	_____	_____	_____	_____	_____

2   **Conjuguez**   Form a new sentence using the cue you hear as the subject. Repeat the correct response after the speaker. (*6 items*)

> **Modèle**
>
> *You hear:* Je ne fais jamais la cuisine. (vous)
> *You say:* Vous ne faites jamais la cuisine.

3   **Complétez**   You will hear the subject of a sentence. Complete the sentence using a form of **faire** and the cue in your lab manual. Repeat the correct response after the speaker.

> **Modèle**
>
> *You hear:* Mon cousin
> *You see:* vélo
> *You say:* Mon cousin fait du vélo.

1. baseball   3. cuisine   5. randonnée

2. camping   4. jogging   6. ski

4   **Complétez**   Listen to this story and write the missing verbs in your lab manual.

Je m'appelle Aurélien. Ma famille et moi sommes très sportifs. Mon père (1) _____ du ski de

compétition. Il (2) _____ aussi de la randonnée en montagne avec mon oncle. Ma mère

(3) _____ du cheval. Son frère et sa sœur (4) _____ du foot. Mon grand frère et moi

(5) _____ du volley à l'école et de la planche à voile. Je (6) _____ aussi du tennis. Ma

sœur et notre cousine (7) _____ du golf. Et vous, que (8) _____-vous comme sport?

5A.2 Irregular -ir verbs

1 **Conjuguez** Form a new sentence using the cue you hear as the subject. Repeat the correct answer after the speaker.

> **Modèle**
>
> *You hear:* Vous ne dormez pas! (tu)
> *You say:* Tu ne dors pas!

1. (nous)   2. (toi et ton frère)   3. (ils)   4. (mon chat)   5. (les sandwichs)   6. (leurs chevaux)

2 **Identifiez** Listen to each sentence and write the infinitive of the verb you hear.

> **Modèle**
>
> *You hear:* L'équipe court au stade Grandjean.
> *You write:* courir

1. _____   5. _____
2. _____   6. _____
3. _____   7. _____
4. _____   8. _____

3 **Questions** Answer each question you hear using the cue in your lab manual. Repeat the correct answer after the speaker.

> **Modèle**
>
> *You hear:* Avec qui tu cours aujourd'hui?
> *You see:* Sarah
> *You say:* Je cours avec Sarah.

1. chez ma tante   2. plus tard   3. les enfants   4. mon ami   5. le chocolat   6. une demi-heure

4 **Les activités** Listen to each statement and write the number of the statement below the drawing it describes. There are more statements than there are drawings.

a. _____

b. _____

c. _____

d. _____   e. _____   f. _____

Unité 5
Leçon 5B

ESPACE CONTEXTES

---

1   **Le temps**   Listen to each statement and write the number of the statement below the drawing it describes. There are more statements than there are drawings.

a. _____

b. _____

c. _____

d. _____

---

2   **Identifiez**   You will hear a series of words. Write the word that does not belong in each series.

1. _____   4. _____

2. _____   5. _____

3. _____   6. _____

---

3   **Questions**   Answer each question you hear using the cues in your lab manual. Repeat the correct response after the speaker.

> **Modèle**
>
> *You hear:* Qu'est-ce qu'on va faire cet été?
> *You see:* faire du camping et une randonnée
> *You say:* Cet été, on va faire du camping et
>   une randonnée.

1. au printemps
2. le 1er février
3. aller souvent au cinéma
4. aimer bricoler
5. aller à un spectacle
6. l'été

LES SONS ET LES LETTRES

Open vs. closed vowels: Part 1

You have already learned that é is pronounced like the vowel *a* in the English word *cake*. This is a closed e sound.

> étudiant   agréable   nationalité   enchanté

The letter combinations -er and -ez at the end of a word are pronounced the same way, as is the vowel sound in single-syllable words ending in -es.

> travailler   avez   mes   les

The vowels spelled è and ê are pronounced like the vowel in the English word *pet*, as is an e followed by a double consonant. These are open e sounds.

> répète   première   pêche   italienne

The vowel sound in *pet* may also be spelled et, ai, or ei.

> secret   français   fait   seize

Compare these pairs of words. To make the vowel sound in *cake*, your mouth should be slightly more closed than when you make the vowel sound in *pet*.

> mes   mais   ces   cette   théâtre   thème

---

1   **Prononcez**   Répétez les mots suivants à voix haute.

1. thé	4. été	7. degrés	10. discret
2. lait	5. neige	8. anglais	11. treize
3. belle	6. aider	9. cassette	12. mauvais

---

2   **Articulez**   Répétez les phrases suivantes à voix haute.

1. Hélène est très discrète.
2. Céleste achète un vélo laid.
3. Il neige souvent en février et en décembre.
4. Désirée est canadienne; elle n'est pas française.

---

3   **Dictons**   Répétez les dictons à voix haute.

1. Péché avoué est à demi pardonné.
2. Qui sème le vent récolte la tempête.

---

4   **Dictée**   You will hear eight sentences. Each will be read twice. Listen carefully and write what you hear.

1. _____
2. _____
3. _____
4. _____
5. _____
6. _____
7. _____
8. _____

ESPACE STRUCTURES

5B.1 Numbers 101 and higher

1 **Calcul** Listen carefully and choose the result that corresponds to each equation.

_____ a. 1.031   _____ e. 500.000

_____ b. 901   _____ f. 200

_____ c. 4.300   _____ g. 3

_____ d. 459   _____ h. 333

2 **Les prix** Listen to each statement and write the correct price next to each object.

1. le palm: _____ €

2. la maison: _____ €

3. l'équipe de baseball: _____ €

4. les cours de tennis: _____ €

5. une randonnée à cheval d'une semaine: _____ €

6. l'ordinateur: _____ €

3 **Le sport** Look at the number of members of sporting clubs in France. Listen to these statements and decide whether each statement is **vrai** or **faux**.

	Nombre de membres
basket-ball	427.000
football	2.066.000
golf	325.000
handball	319.000
judo	577.000
natation	214.000
rugby	253.000
tennis	1.068.000

	Vrai	Faux
1.	○	○
2.	○	○
3.	○	○
4.	○	○
5.	○	○
6.	○	○

4 **Questions** Answer each question you hear using the cue in your lab manual. Repeat the correct response after the speaker.

> **Modèle**
> _You hear:_ Combien de personnes pratiquent la natation en France?
> _You see:_ 214.000
> _You say:_ Deux cent quatorze mille personnes pratiquent la natation en France.

1. 371
2. 880
3. 101
4. 412
5. 1.630
6. 129

5B.2 Spelling change -er verbs

1 Décrivez You will hear two statements for each drawing. Choose the one that corresponds to the drawing.

1. a.   b.   2. a.   b.   3. a.   b.   4. a.   b.

2 Conjuguez Form a new sentence using the cue you hear as the subject. Repeat the correct response after the speaker. (*6 items*)

Modèle

You hear: Vous ne payez pas maintenant? (tu)
You say: Tu ne payes/paies pas maintenant?

3 Transformez Change each sentence from the immediate future to the present. Repeat the correct answer after the speaker. (*6 items*)

Modèle

You hear: Ils vont envoyer leurs papiers.
You say: Ils envoient leurs papiers.

4 Identifiez Listen to each sentence and write the infinitive of the verb you hear.

Modèle

You hear: Monique promène le chien de sa sœur.
You write: promener

1. _____ 5. _____
2. _____ 6. _____
3. _____ 7. _____
4. _____ 8. _____

Unité 6   Leçon 6A

1 **Logique ou illogique?** You will hear some statements. Decide if each one is **logique** or **illogique**.

	Logique	Illogique			Logique	Illogique
1.	○	○		5.	○	○
2.	○	○		6.	○	○
3.	○	○		7.	○	○
4.	○	○		8.	○	○

2 **Choisissez** For each drawing you will hear three statements. Choose the one that corresponds to the drawing.

1. a.   b.   c.   2. a.   b.   c.   3. a.   b.   c.   4. a.   b.   c.

3 **L'anniversaire** Listen as Véronique talks about a party she has planned. Then answer the questions in your lab manual.

1. Pour qui Véronique organise-t-elle une fête?

_____

2. Quand est cette fête?

_____

3. Pourquoi est-ce qu'on organise cette fête?

_____

4. Qui Véronique invite-t-elle?

_____

5. Qui achète le cadeau?

_____

6. Qui apporte de la musique?

_____

7. Le gâteau est à quoi?

_____

8. Qu'est-ce que les invités vont faire à la fête?

_____

Unité 6 Lab Activities   **41**

LES SONS ET LES LETTRES

Open vs. closed vowels: Part 2

The letter combinations **au** and **eau** are pronounced like the vowel sound in the English word *coat*, but without the glide heard in English. These are closed o sounds.

     ch**au**d   **au**ssi   be**au**coup   tabl**eau**

When the letter o is followed by a consonant sound, it is usually pronounced like the vowel in the English word *raw*. This is an open o sound.

     h**o**mme   téléph**o**ne   **o**rdinateur   **o**range

When the letter o occurs as the last sound of a word or is followed by a z sound, such as a single s between two vowels, it is usually pronounced with the closed o sound.

     tr**o**p   hér**o**s   r**o**se   ch**o**se

When the letter o has an **accent circonflexe**, it is usually pronounced with the closed o sound.

     dr**ô**le   bient**ô**t   p**ô**le   c**ô**té

1   **Prononcez** Répétez les mots suivants à voix haute.

1. rôle	4. chaud	7. oiseau	10. nouveau
2. porte	5. prose	8. encore	11. restaurant
3. dos	6. gros	9. mauvais	12. bibliothèque

2   **Articulez** Répétez les phrases suivantes à voix haute.

1. En automne, on n'a pas trop chaud.
2. Aurélie a une bonne note en biologie.
3. Votre colocataire est d'origine japonaise?
4. Sophie aime beaucoup l'informatique et la psychologie.
5. Nos copains mangent au restaurant marocain aujourd'hui.
6. Comme cadeau, Robert et Corinne vont préparer un gâteau.

3   **Dictons** Répétez les dictons à voix haute.

1. Tout nouveau, tout beau.   2. La fortune vient en dormant.

4   **Dictée** You will hear six sentences. Each will be read twice. Listen carefully and write what you hear.

1. _____
2. _____
3. _____
4. _____
5. _____
6. _____

ESPACE STRUCTURES

6A.1 Demonstrative adjectives

1 **La fête** You are at a party. Listen to what the guests have to say about the party, and mark an **X** in the column of the demonstrative adjective you hear.

> **Modèle**
>
> *You hear:* J'adore ces petits gâteaux au chocolat.
> *You mark:* an **X** under **ces**

	ce	cet	cette	ces
Modèle	_____	_____	_____	X
1.	_____	_____	_____	_____
2.	_____	_____	_____	_____
3.	_____	_____	_____	_____
4.	_____	_____	_____	_____
5.	_____	_____	_____	_____
6.	_____	_____	_____	_____
7.	_____	_____	_____	_____
8.	_____	_____	_____	_____

2 **Changez** Form a sentence using the cue you hear. Repeat the correct answer after the speaker. (6 *items*)

> **Modèle**
>
> des biscuits
> Je vais acheter *ces biscuits.*

3 **Transformez** Form a new sentence using the cue in your lab manual. Repeat the correct response after the speaker.

> **Modèle**
>
> *You hear:* J'aime ces bonbons.
> *You see:* fête
> *You say:* J'aime *cette* fête.

1. dessert   3. hôte   5. eaux minérales
2. glace   4. mariage   6. sandwich

4 **Demandez** Answer each question you hear in the negative. Repeat the correct answer after the speaker. (6 *items*)

> **Modèle**
>
> Tu aimes cette glace?
> Non, je n'aime pas *cette glace-ci,* j'aime *cette glace-là.*

6A.2 The passé composé with avoir

1 **Identifiez** Listen to each sentence and decide whether the verb is in the **présent** or the **passé composé**. Mark an **X** in the appropriate column.

> **Modèle**
> *You hear:* Tu as fait tout ça?
> *You mark:* an **X** under **passé composé**

	présent	passé composé
Modèle	_____	X
1.	_____	_____
2.	_____	_____
3.	_____	_____
4.	_____	_____
5.	_____	_____
6.	_____	_____
7.	_____	_____
8.	_____	_____

2 **Changez** Change each sentence from the **présent** to the **passé composé**. Repeat the correct answer after the speaker. (*8 items*)

> **Modèle**
> J'apporte la glace.
> J'ai apporté la glace.

3 **Questions** Answer each question you hear using the cue in your lab manual. Repeat the correct response after the speaker.

> **Modèle**
> *You hear:* Où as-tu acheté ce gâteau?
> *You see:* au marché
> *You say:* J'ai acheté ce gâteau au marché.

1. avec Élisabeth   3. oui   5. non   7. oui
2. Marc et Audrey   4. non   6. oui   8. Christine et Alain

4 **C'est prêt?** Listen to this conversation between Virginie and Caroline. Make a list of what is already done and a list of what still needs to be prepared.

Est déjà préparé _____

_____

N'est pas encore préparé _____

_____

Unité 6

Leçon 6B

1 **Logique ou illogique?** Listen to each statement and indicate if it is **logique** or **illogique**.

	Logique	Illogique			Logique	Illogique
1.	○	○		5.	○	○
2.	○	○		6.	○	○
3.	○	○		7.	○	○
4.	○	○		8.	○	○

2 **Choisissez** Listen as each person talks about the clothing he or she needs to buy, then choose the activity for which the clothing would be appropriate.

1. a. voyager en été   b. faire du ski en hiver
2. a. marcher à la montagne   b. aller à la piscine l'été
3. a. faire de la planche à voile   b. faire du jogging
4. a. aller à l'opéra   b. jouer au golf
5. a. partir en voyage   b. faire une randonnée
6. a. faire une promenade   b. faire de l'aérobic

3 **Questions** Respond to each question saying the opposite. Repeat the correct answer after the speaker. (*6 items*)

> **Modèle**
> Cette écharpe est-elle longue?
> Non, *cette écharpe est courte.*

4 **Quelle couleur?** Respond to each question using the cues in your lab manual. Repeat the correct answer after the speaker.

> **Modèle**
> *You hear:* De quelle couleur est cette chemise?
> *You see:* vert
> *You say:* Cette chemise est verte.

1. gris   2. bleu   3. violet   4. marron   5. blanc   6. jaune

5 **Décrivez** You will hear some questions. Look at the drawing and write the answer to each question.

Sylvie   Corinne

1. _____
2. _____
3. _____
4. _____

LES SONS ET LES LETTRES

Open vs. closed vowels: Part 3

The letter combination eu can be pronounced two different ways, open and closed. Compare the pronunciation of the vowel sounds in these words.

cheveux   neveu   heure   meilleur

When eu is followed by a pronounced consonant, it has an open sound. The open eu sound does not exist in English. To pronounce it, say è with your lips only slightly rounded.

peur   jeune   chanteur   beurre

The letter combination œu is usually pronounced with an open eu sound.

sœur   bœuf   œuf   chœur

When eu is the last sound of a syllable, it has a closed vowel sound, similar to the vowel sound in the English word *full*. While this exact sound does not exist in English, you can make the closed eu sound by saying é with your lips rounded.

deux   bleu   peu   mieux

When eu is followed by a *z* sound, such as a single s between two vowels, it is usually pronounced with the closed eu sound.

chanteuse   généreuse   sérieuse   curieuse

1   **Prononcez** Répétez les mots suivants à voix haute.

    1. leur   4. vieux   7. monsieur   10. tailleur

    2. veuve   5. curieux   8. coiffeuse   11. vendeuse

    3. neuf   6. acteur   9. ordinateur   12. couleur

2   **Articulez** Répétez les phrases suivantes à voix haute.

    1. Le professeur Heudier a soixante-deux ans.

    2. Est-ce que Matthieu est jeune ou vieux?

    3. Monsieur Eustache est un chanteur fabuleux.

    4. Eugène a les yeux bleus et les cheveux bruns.

3   **Dictons** Répétez les dictons à voix haute.

    1. Qui vole un œuf, vole un bœuf.

    2. Les conseilleurs ne sont pas les payeurs.

4   **Dictée** You will hear four sentences. Each will be read twice. Listen carefully and write what you hear.

    1. _____

    2. _____

    3. _____

    4. _____

ESPACE STRUCTURES

6B.1 Indirect object pronouns

1 **Choisissez** Listen to each question and choose the most logical response.

1. a. Oui, je lui ai montré ma robe.
   b. Oui, je leur ai montré ma robe.
2. a. Oui, je leur ai envoyé un cadeau.
   b. Oui, je vous ai envoyé un cadeau.
3. a. Non, je ne leur ai pas téléphoné.
   b. Non, je ne lui ai pas téléphoné.
4. a. Oui, nous allons leur donner cette cravate.
   b. Oui, nous allons lui donner cette cravate.
5. a. Non, il ne m'a pas prêté sa moto.
   b. Non, il ne t'a pas prêté sa moto.
6. a. Oui, ils vous ont répondu.
   b. Oui, ils nous ont répondu.

2 **Transformez** Aurore has been shopping. Say for whom she bought these items using indirect object pronouns. Repeat the correct answer after the speaker. (6 *items*)

Modèle
Aurore achète un livre à Audrey.
Aurore lui achète un livre.

3 **Questions** Answer each question you hear using the cue in your lab manual. Repeat the correct response after the speaker.

Modèle
You hear: Tu poses souvent des questions à tes parents?
You see: oui
You say: Oui, je leur pose souvent des questions.

1. non
2. une écharpe
3. des gants
4. non
5. non
6. à 8 heures

6B.2 Regular and irregular -re verbs

1   **Identifiez** Listen to each sentence and write the infinitive form of the verb you hear.

> **Modèle**
>
> _You hear:_ L'enfant sourit à ses parents.
> _You write:_ sourire

1. _____
2. _____
3. _____
4. _____

5. _____
6. _____
7. _____
8. _____

2   **Changez** Form a new sentence using the cue you hear as the subject. Repeat the sentence after the speaker. (_6 items_)

> **Modèle**
>
> _You hear:_ Elle attend le bus. (nous)
> _You say:_ Nous attendons le bus.

3   **Répondez** Answer each question you hear using the cue in your lab manual. Repeat the correct answer after the speaker.

> **Modèle**
>
> _You hear:_ Quel jour est-ce que tu rends visite à
>   tes parents?
> _You see:_ le dimanche
> _You say:_ Je rends visite à mes parents
>   le dimanche.

1. non   3. oui   5. le mois dernier
2. une robe   4. non   6. trois

4   **Complétez** Listen to this description and write the missing words.

Le mercredi, je (1) _____ à mes grands-parents. Je ne (2) _____

pas, je prends le train. Je (3) _____ à Soissons, où mes grands-parents

(4) _____. Quand ils (5) _____ le train arriver, ils

(6) _____. Nous rentrons chez eux; nous ne (7) _____

pas de temps et nous déjeunons tout de suite. L'après-midi passe vite et il est déjà l'heure de reprendre le

train. Je (8) _____ à mes grands-parents de leur (9) _____

bientôt. Ils ne (10) _____ pas non plus, alors j'appelle un taxi pour aller prendre

mon train.

Unité 7

ESPACE CONTEXTES

1 **Identifiez** You will hear a series of words. Write the word that does not belong to each series.

1. _____ 5. _____

2. _____ 6. _____

3. _____ 7. _____

4. _____ 8. _____

2 **Décrivez** For each drawing you will hear two statements. Choose the one that corresponds to the drawing.

1. a.   b.   2. a.   b.   3. a.   b.

3 **À l'agence** Listen to the conversation between Éric and a travel agent. Then read the statements in your lab manual and decide whether they are **vrai** or **faux**.

	Vrai	Faux
1. Éric pense partir en vacances une semaine.	O	O
2. Éric aime skier et jouer au golf.	O	O
3. Pour Éric, la campagne est une excellente idée.	O	O
4. Éric préfère la mer.	O	O
5. Il n'y a pas de plage en Corse.	O	O
6. Éric prend ses vacances la dernière semaine de juin.	O	O
7. Le vol de retour pour l'aéroport d'Ajaccio est le 9 juin.	O	O
8. Le billet d'avion aller-retour coûte 120 euros.	O	O

LES SONS ET LES LETTRES

Diacriticals for meaning

Some French words with different meanings have nearly identical spellings except for a diacritical mark (**accent**). Sometimes a diacritical does not affect pronunciation at all.

ou	où	a	à
or	*where*	*has*	*to, at*

Sometimes, you can clearly hear the difference between the words.

côte	côté	sale	salé
coast	*side*	*dirty*	*salty*

Very often, two similar-looking words are different parts of speech. Many similar-looking word pairs are those with and without an -é at the end.

âge	âgé	entre	entré (entrer)
age (n.)	*elderly* (adj.)	*between* (prep.)	*entered* (p.p.)

In such instances, context should make their meaning clear.

Tu as quel **âge**?	C'est un homme **âgé**.
How old are you? / What is your age?	*He's an elderly man.*

---

1   **Prononcez**   Répétez les mots suivants à voix haute.

1. la (*the*)   là (*there*)
2. êtes (*are*)   étés (*summers*)
3. jeune (*young*)   jeûne (*fasting*)
4. pêche (*peach*)   pêché (*fished*)

---

2   **Articulez**   Répétez les phrases suivantes à voix haute.

1. J'habite dans une ferme (*farm*).
   Le magasin est fermé (*closed*).
2. Les animaux mangent du maïs (*corn*).
   Je suis suisse, mais il est belge.
3. Est-ce que tu es prête?
   J'ai prêté ma voiture à Marcel.
4. La lampe est à côté de la chaise.
   J'adore la côte ouest de la France.

---

3   **Dictons**   Répétez les dictons à voix haute.

1. À vos marques, prêts, partez!
2. C'est un prêté pour un rendu.

---

4   **Dictée**   You will hear six sentences. Each will be said twice. Listen carefully and write what you hear.

1. _____
2. _____
3. _____
4. _____
5. _____
6. _____

ESPACE STRUCTURES

7A.1 The passé composé with être

1 **Choisissez** Listen to each sentence and indicate whether the verb is conjugated with **avoir** or **être**.

	avoir	être
1.	○	○
2.	○	○
3.	○	○
4.	○	○
5.	○	○
6.	○	○
7.	○	○
8.	○	○

2 **Changez** Change each sentence from the **présent** to the **passé composé**. Repeat the correct answer after the speaker. (*8 items*)

> **Modèle**
>
> Vous restez au Québec trois semaines.
> *Vous êtes resté(e)(s) au Québec trois semaines.*

3 **Questions** Answer each question you hear using the cue in your lab manual. Repeat the correct response after the speaker.

> **Modèle**
>
> *You hear:* Qui est parti en vacances avec toi?
> *You see:* Caroline
> *You say: Caroline est partie en vacances avec moi.*

1. au Canada   3. mercredi   5. trois jours
2. non   4. par la Suisse et par l'Italie   6. oui

4 **Ça va?** Listen to Patrick and Magali and answer the questions in your lab manual.

1. Est-ce que Patrick est fatigué? _____

2. Avec qui Magali est-elle sortie? _____

3. Où sont-ils allés? _____

4. Qui Magali a-t-elle rencontré? _____

5. Qu'ont-ils fait ensuite? _____

6. À quelle heure Magali est-elle rentrée chez elle? _____

7A.2 Direct object pronouns

1 **Choisissez** Listen to each question and choose the most logical answer.

1. a. Oui, je la regarde.
   b. Oui, je les regarde.
2. a. Non, je ne l'ai pas.
   b. Non, je ne les ai pas.
3. a. Non, je ne l'attends pas.
   b. Non, je ne t'attends pas.
4. a. Oui, nous vous écoutons.
   b. Oui, nous les écoutons.
5. a. Oui, je l'ai appris.
   b. Oui, je les ai appris.
6. a. Oui, ils vont te chercher.
   b. Oui, ils vont nous chercher.
7. a. Oui, je vais les acheter.
   b. Oui, je vais l'acheter.
8. a. Oui, je l'ai acheté.
   b. Oui, je les ai achetés.

2 **Changez** Restate each sentence you hear using a direct object pronoun. Repeat the correct answer after the speaker. (8 *items*)

> **Modèle**
> Nous regardons la télévision.
> Nous *la regardons.*

3 **Répondez** Answer each question you hear using the cue in your lab manual. Repeat the correct answer after the speaker.

> **Modèle**
> Qui va t'attendre à la gare? (mes parents)
> Mes parents vont *m'attendre à la gare.*

1. au marché   3. oui   5. sur Internet
2. ce matin   4. midi   6. oui

4 **Questions** Answer each question you hear in the negative. Repeat the correct response after the speaker. (6 *items*)

> **Modèle**
> Est-ce que vos grands-parents vous ont attendus?
> Non, ils *ne nous ont pas attendus.*

Unité 7

ESPACE CONTEXTES

1 **Identifiez** You will hear a series of words. Write the word that does not belong in each series.

1. _____   5. _____

2. _____   6. _____

3. _____   7. _____

4. _____   8. _____

2 **La réception** Look at the drawing and listen to each statement. Then decide if the statement is **vrai** or **faux**.

	Vrai	Faux
1.	○	○
2.	○	○
3.	○	○
4.	○	○
5.	○	○
6.	○	○
7.	○	○
8.	○	○

3 **Complétez** Listen to this description and write the missing words in your lab manual.

Pour les étudiants, les (1) _____ sont très bon marché quand ils ont envie de

voyager. Généralement, elles ont de grandes (2) _____ avec trois, quatre ou cinq

(3) _____. C'est très sympa quand vous partez (4) _____

avec vos amis. Les auberges sont souvent petites et il faut faire des (5) _____.

Dans ma ville, l'auberge a une toute petite (6) _____, vingt chambres et trois

(7) _____. Il n'y a pas d' (8) _____.

LES SONS ET LES LETTRES

ti, sti, and ssi

The letters **ti** followed by a consonant are pronounced like the English word *tea*, but without the puff released in the English pronunciation.

    ac**ti**f   pe**ti**t   **ti**gre   u**ti**les

When the letter combination **ti** is followed by a vowel sound, it is often pronounced like the sound linking the English words *miss you*.

    dic**ti**onnaire   pa**ti**ent   ini**ti**al   addi**ti**on

Regardless of whether it is followed by a consonant or a vowel, the letter combination **sti** is pronounced *stee*, as in the English word *steep*.

    ge**sti**on   que**sti**on   Séba**sti**en   arti**sti**que

The letter combination **ssi** followed by another vowel or a consonant is usually pronounced like the sound linking the English words *miss you*.

    pa**ssi**on   expre**ssi**on   mi**ssi**on   profe**ssi**on

Words that end in **-sion** or **-tion** are often cognates with English words, but they are pronounced quite differently. In French, these words are never pronounced with a *sh* sound.

    compre**ssi**on   na**ti**on   atten**ti**on   addi**ti**on

---

1   **Prononcez** Répétez les mots suivants à voix haute.

    1. artiste   3. réservation   5. position   7. possession   9. compassion

    2. mission   4. impatient   6. initiative   8. nationalité   10. possible

---

2   **Articulez** Répétez les phrases suivantes à voix haute.

    1. L'addition, s'il vous plaît.
    2. Christine est optimiste et active.
    3. Elle a fait une bonne première impression.
    4. Laëtitia est impatiente parce qu'elle est fatiguée.
    5. Tu cherches des expressions idiomatiques dans le dictionnaire.

---

3   **Dictons** Répétez les dictons à voix haute.

    1. De la discussion jaillit la lumière.   2. Il n'est de règle sans exception.

---

4   **Dictée** You will hear six sentences. Each will be said twice. Listen carefully and write what you hear.

    1. _____

    2. _____

    3. _____

    4. _____

    5. _____

    6. _____

ESPACE STRUCTURES

7B.1 Adverbs

1 **Complétez** Listen to each statement and circle the word or phrase that best completes it.

1. a. couramment   b. faiblement   c. difficilement
2. a. gentiment   b. fortement   c. joliment
3. a. rapidement   b. malheureusement   c. lentement
4. a. constamment   b. brillamment   c. utilement
5. a. rapidement   b. fréquemment   c. patiemment
6. a. activement   b. franchement   c. nerveusement

2 **Changez** Form a new sentence by changing the adjective in your lab manual to an adverb. Repeat the correct answer after the speaker.

> **Modèle**
>
> *You hear:* Julie étudie.
> *You see:* sérieux
> *You say:* Julie étudie sérieusement.

1. poli
2. rapide
3. différent
4. courant
5. patient
6. prudent

3 **Répondez** Answer each question you hear in the negative, using the cue in the lab manual. Repeat the correct answer after the speaker.

> **Modèle**
>
> *You hear:* Ils vont très souvent au cinéma?
> *You see:* rarement
> *You say:* Non, ils vont rarement au cinéma.

1. mal
2. tard
3. rarement
4. méchamment
5. vite
6. facilement

7B.2 Formation of the **imparfait**

1 **Identifiez** Listen to each sentence and circle the verb tense you hear.

1. a. présent   b. imparfait   c. passé composé
2. a. présent   b. imparfait   c. passé composé
3. a. présent   b. imparfait   c. passé composé
4. a. présent   b. imparfait   c. passé composé
5. a. présent   b. imparfait   c. passé composé
6. a. présent   b. imparfait   c. passé composé
7. a. présent   b. imparfait   c. passé composé
8. a. présent   b. imparfait   c. passé composé
9. a. présent   b. imparfait   c. passé composé
10. a. présent   b. imparfait   c. passé composé

2 **Changez** Form a new sentence using the cue you hear. Repeat the correct answer after the speaker. (6 *items*)

> **Modèle**
>
> Je dînais à huit heures. (nous)
> *Nous dînions à huit heures.*

3 **Répondez** Answer each question you hear using the cue in your lab manual. Then repeat the correct response after the speaker.

> **Modèle**
>
> *You hear:* Qu'est-ce que tu faisais quand tu avais 15 ans?
> *You see:* aller au lycée Condorcet
> *You say:* J'allais au lycée Condorcet.

1. jouer au tennis avec François
2. aller à la mer près de Cannes
3. étudier à la bibliothèque de l'université
4. sortir au restaurant avec des amis
5. finir nos devoirs et regarder la télé
6. sortir le chien et jouer au foot
7. partir skier dans les Alpes
8. sortir avec des amis et aller au cinéma

Unité 8

ESPACE CONTEXTES

1   **Décrivez**   Listen to each sentence and write its number below the drawing of the household item mentioned.

a. _____   b. _____   c. _____

d. _____   e. _____   f. _____

2   **Identifiez**   You will hear a series of words. Write the word that does not belong in each series.

1. _____   5. _____

2. _____   6. _____

3. _____   7. _____

4. _____   8. _____

3   **Logique ou illogique?**   You will hear some statements. Decide if they are **logique** or **illogique**.

	Logique	Illogique			Logique	Illogique
1.	○	○		5.	○	○
2.	○	○		6.	○	○
3.	○	○		7.	○	○
4.	○	○		8.	○	○

LES SONS ET LES LETTRES

s and ss

You've already learned that an **s** at the end of a word is usually silent.

lavabo**s** copain**s** va**s** placard**s**

An **s** at the beginning of a word, before a consonant, or after a pronounced consonant is pronounced like the *s* in the English word *set*.

soir **s**alon **s**tudio ab**s**olument

A double *s* is pronounced like the *ss* in the English word *kiss*.

gro**ss**e a**ss**ez intére**ss**ant rou**ss**e

An **s** at the end of a word is often pronounced when the following word begins with a vowel sound. An **s** in a liaison sounds like a *z*, like the *s* in the English word *rose*.

très élégant trois hommes

The other instance where the French **s** has a *z* sound is when there is a single **s** between two vowels within the same word. The **s** is pronounced like the *s* in the English word *music*.

mu**s**ée amu**s**ant oi**s**eau be**s**oin

These words look alike, but have different meanings. Compare the pronunciations of each word pair.

poi**s**on poi**ss**on dé**s**ert de**ss**ert

1 **Prononcez** Répétez les mots suivants à voix haute.

1. sac
2. triste
3. suisse
4. chose
5. bourse
6. passer
7. surprise
8. assister
9. magasin
10. expressions
11. sénégalaise
12. sérieusement

2 **Articulez** Répétez les phrases suivantes à voix haute.

1. Le spectacle est très amusant et la chanteuse est superbe.
2. Est-ce que vous habitez dans une résidence universitaire?
3. De temps en temps, Suzanne assiste à l'inauguration d'expositions au musée.
4. Heureusement, mes professeurs sont sympathiques, sociables et très sincères.

3 **Dictons** Répétez les dictons à voix haute.

1. Si jeunesse savait, si vieillesse pouvait.
2. Les oiseaux de même plumage s'assemblent sur le même rivage.

4 **Dictée** You will hear six sentences. Each will be said twice. Listen carefully and write what you hear.

1. _____
2. _____
3. _____
4. _____
5. _____
6. _____

ESPACE STRUCTURES

8A.1 The passé composé vs. the imparfait (Part 1)

1 **Identifiez** Listen to each sentence in the past tense and indicate which category best describes it.

1. a. habitual action   b. specific completed action   c. description of a physical/mental state
2. a. habitual action   b. specific completed action   c. description of a physical/mental state
3. a. habitual action   b. specific completed action   c. description of a physical/mental state
4. a. habitual action   b. specific completed action   c. description of a physical/mental state
5. a. habitual action   b. specific completed action   c. description of a physical/mental state
6. a. habitual action   b. specific completed action   c. description of a physical/mental state
7. a. habitual action   b. specific completed action   c. description of a physical/mental state
8. a. habitual action   b. specific completed action   c. description of a physical/mental state
9. a. habitual action   b. specific completed action   c. description of a physical/mental state
10. a. habitual action   b. specific completed action   c. description of a physical/mental state

2 **Choisissez** Listen to each question and choose the most logical answer.

1. a. Il pleuvait et il faisait froid.
   b. Il a plu et il a fait froid.
2. a. J'ai joué au volley avec mes amis.
   b. Je jouais au volley avec mes amis.
3. a. Nous sommes allés au musée.
   b. Nous allions au musée.
4. a. Super! On a dansé toute la nuit.
   b. Super! On dansait toute la nuit.
5. a. Je les mettais dans ton sac.
   b. Je les ai mises dans ton sac.
6. a. Il a passé les vacances d'été en Espagne.
   b. Il passait les vacances d'été en Espagne.

3 **Complétez** Complete each sentence you hear in the **passé composé** or the **imparfait** using the cue in your lab manual. Repeat the correct response after the speaker.

> **Modèle**
> *You hear:* Ma petite amie adore danser maintenant, mais quand elle était au lycée...
> *You see:* préférer chanter
> *You say: elle préférait chanter.*

1. manger un sandwich
2. jouer au football
3. sortir tous les soirs
4. prendre un taxi
5. nettoyer le garage
6. porter des jupes

8A.2 The passé composé vs. the imparfait (Part 2)

1 **Complétez** Listen to each phrase and complete it using the cues in your lab manual. Repeat the correct response after the speaker.

> **Modèle**
>
> _You hear:_ Elle regardait la télé quand...
> _You see:_ son frère / sortir la poubelle
> _You say:_ Elle regardait la télé quand son frère a sorti la poubelle.

1. papa / rentrer
2. son petit ami / téléphoner
3. mes sœurs / dormir
4. la cafetière / tomber
5. vous / être dans le jardin
6. nous / vivre au Sénégal

2 **Changez** Change each sentence you hear in the present tense to the appropriate past tense. Repeat the correct response after the speaker. (_8 items_)

> **Modèle**
>
> D'habitude, je sors à huit heures du matin.
> D'habitude, je sortais à huit heures du matin.

3 **Répondez** Answer each question you hear using the cue in your lab manual. Repeat the correct response after the speaker.

> **Modèle**
>
> _You hear:_ Qu'est-ce que tu lisais quand tu avais neuf ans?
> _You see:_ des bandes dessinées
> _You say:_ Je lisais des bandes dessinées.

1. des frites
2. rendre visite à mes grands-parents
3. au centre commercial
4. aller au centre-ville
5. non, dans une grande maison
6. une robe noire

Unité 8

ESPACE CONTEXTES

Leçon 8B

1 **Logique ou illogique?** Listen to these statements and indicate whether they are **logique** or **illogique**.

	Logique	Illogique
1.	○	○
2.	○	○
3.	○	○
4.	○	○
5.	○	○
6.	○	○
7.	○	○
8.	○	○

2 **Les tâches ménagères** Martin is a good housekeeper and does everything that needs to be done in the house. Listen to each statement and decide what he did. Then, repeat the correct answer after the speaker. (*6 items*)

> **Modèle**
> Les vêtements étaient sales.
> Alors, il a fait la lessive.

3 **Décrivez** Julie has invited a few friends over. When her friends are gone, she goes in the kitchen. Look at the drawing and write the answer to each question you hear.

1. _____
2. _____
3. _____
4. _____

LES SONS ET LES LETTRES

Semi-vowels

French has three semi-vowels. Semi-vowels are sounds that are produced in much the same way as vowels, but also have many properties in common with consonants. Semi-vowels are also sometimes referred to as *glides* because they glide from or into the vowel they accompany.

hier   **chien**   **soif**   **nuit**

The semi-vowel that occurs in the word **bien** is very much like the *y* in the English word *yes*. It is usually spelled with an **i** or a **y** (pronounced *ee*), then glides into the following sound. This semi-vowel sound may also be spelled **ll** after an **i**.

nation   **balayer**   **bien**   **brillant**

The semi-vowel that occurs in the word **soif** is like the *w* in the English word *was*. It usually begins with **o** or **ou**, then glides into the following vowel.

trois   **froid**   **oui**   **Louis**

The third semi-vowel sound occurs in the word **nuit**. It is spelled with the vowel **u**, as in the French word **tu**, then glides into the following sound.

lui   **suis**   **cruel**   **intellectuel**

1   **Prononcez** Répétez les mots suivants à voix haute.

1. oui
2. taille
3. suisse
4. fille
5. mois
6. cruel
7. minuit
8. jouer
9. cuisine
10. juillet
11. échouer
12. croissant

2   **Articulez** Répétez les phrases suivantes à voix haute.

1. Voici trois poissons noirs.
2. Louis et sa famille sont suisses.
3. Parfois, Grégoire fait de la cuisine chinoise.
4. Aujourd'hui, Matthieu et Damien vont travailler.
5. Françoise a besoin de faire ses devoirs d'histoire.
6. La fille de Monsieur Poirot va conduire pour la première fois.

3   **Dictons** Répétez les dictons à voix haute.

1. La nuit, tous les chats sont gris.
2. Vouloir, c'est pouvoir.

4   **Dictée** You will hear six sentences. Each will be said twice. Listen carefully and write what you hear.

1. _____
2. _____
3. _____
4. _____
5. _____
6. _____

ESPACE STRUCTURES

8B.1 The **passé composé** vs. the **imparfait**: Summary

1 **Identifiez** Listen to each statement and identify the verbs in the **imparfait** and the **passé composé**. Write them in the appropriate column.

Modèle

You hear: Quand je suis entrée dans la cuisine, maman faisait la vaisselle.

You write: suis entrée under **passé composé** and faisait under **imparfait**

	Imparfait	Passé composé
Modèle	faisait	suis entrée
1.	_____	_____
2.	_____	_____
3.	_____	_____
4.	_____	_____
5.	_____	_____
6.	_____	_____
7.	_____	_____
8.	_____	_____

2 **Répondez** Answer the questions using cues in your lab manual. Substitute direct object pronouns for the direct object nouns when appropriate. Repeat the correct response after the speaker.

Modèle

You hear: Pourquoi as-tu passé l'aspirateur?
You see: la cuisine / être sale
You say: Je l'ai passé parce que la cuisine était sale.

1. avoir des invités
2. pleuvoir
3. être fatigué
4. avoir soif
5. ranger l'appartement
6. faire beau
7. pendant que Myriam / préparer le repas
8. être malade

3 **Vrai ou faux?** Listen as Coralie tells you about her childhood. Then read the statements in your lab book and decide whether they are **vrai** or **faux**.

	Vrai	Faux
1. Quand elle était petite, Coralie habitait à Paris avec sa famille.	○	○
2. Son père était architecte.	○	○
3. Coralie a des frères et une sœur.	○	○
4. Tous les soirs, Coralie mettait la table.	○	○
5. Sa mère sortait le chien après dîner.	○	○
6. Un jour, ses parents ont tout vendu.	○	○
7. Coralie aime beaucoup habiter près de la mer.	○	○

8B.2 The verbs **savoir** and **connaître**

1 **Connaître ou savoir** You will hear some sentences with a beep in place of the verb. Decide which form of **connaître** or **savoir** should complete each sentence and circle it.

1. a. sais   b. connais
2. a. sait   b. connaît
3. a. savons   b. connaissons
4. a. connaissent   b. savent
5. a. connaissez   b. savez
6. a. connaissons   b. savons

2 **Changez** Listen to the following statements and say that you do the same activities. Repeat the correct answer after the speaker. (6 *items*)

> **Modèle**
>
> Alexandre sait parler chinois.
> Moi aussi, je sais parler chinois.

3 **Répondez** Answer each question using the cue that you hear. Repeat the correct response after the speaker. (6 *items*)

> **Modèle**
>
> Est-ce que tes parents connaissent tes amis? (oui)
> Oui, mes parents connaissent mes amis.

4 **Mon amie** Listen as Salomé describes her roommate Then read the statements in your lab manual and decide whether they are **vrai** or **faux**.

	Vrai	Faux
1. Salomé a connu Christine au bureau.	O	O
2. Christine sait parler russe.	O	O
3. Christine sait danser.	O	O
4. Salomé connaît maintenant des recettes.	O	O
5. Christine sait passer l'aspirateur.	O	O
6. Christine ne sait pas repasser.	O	O

Unité 9

Leçon 9A

1 **Identifiez** Listen to each question and mark an **X** in the appropriate category.

> *Modèle*
> *You hear:* Un steak, qu'est-ce que c'est?
> *You mark:* **X** under **viande**

	viande	poisson	légume(s)	fruit(s)
Modèle	X			
1.				
2.				
3.				
4.				
5.				
6.				
7.				
8.				
9.				
10.				

2 **Quelques suggestions** Listen to each sentence and write the number under the drawing of the food mentioned.

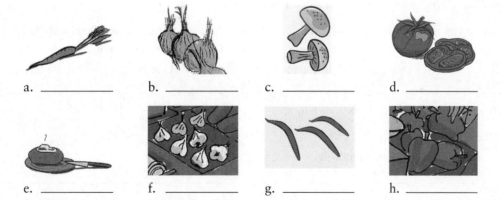

a. _____ b. _____ c. _____ d. _____

e. _____ f. _____ g. _____ h. _____

3 **Au restaurant** You will hear a couple ordering food in a restaurant. Write the items they order in the appropriate category.

	LÉA	THÉO
Pour commencer		
Viande ou poisson		
Légumes		
Dessert		
Boisson		

LES SONS ET LES LETTRES

e caduc and e muet

In Leçon 7, you learned that the vowel e in very short words is pronounced similarly to the *a* in the English word *about*. This sound is called an **e caduc**. An **e caduc** can also occur in longer words and before words beginning with vowel sounds.

| rechercher | devoirs | le haricot | le onze |

An **e caduc** occurs in order to break up clusters of several consonants.

| appartement | quelquefois | poivre vert | gouvernement |

An **e caduc** is sometimes called **e muet** (*mute*). It is often dropped in spoken French.

Tu ne sais pas.   Je veux bien!   C'est un livre intéressant.

An unaccented e before a single consonant sound is often silent unless its omission makes the word difficult to pronounce.

semaine   petit   finalement

An unaccented e at the end of a word is usually silent and often marks a feminine noun or adjective.

fraise   salade   intelligente   jeune

1 Prononcez Répétez les mots suivants à voix haute.

1. vendredi
2. logement
3. exemple
4. devenir
5. tartelette
6. finalement
7. boucherie
8. petits pois
9. pomme de terre
10. malheureusement

2 Articulez Répétez les phrases suivantes à voix haute.

1. Tu ne vas pas prendre de casquette?
2. J'étudie le huitième chapitre maintenant.
3. Il va passer ses vacances en Angleterre.
4. Marc me parle souvent au téléphone.
5. Mercredi, je réserve dans une auberge.
6. Finalement, ce petit logement est bien.

3 Dictons Répétez les dictons à voix haute.

1. L'habit ne fait pas le moine.
2. Le soleil luit pour tout le monde.

4 Dictée You will hear six sentences. Each will be said twice. Listen carefully and write what you hear.

1. _____
2. _____
3. _____
4. _____
5. _____
6. _____

ESPACE STRUCTURES

9A.1 The verb **venir** and the **passé récent**

1   **Identifiez** Listen to each sentence and decide whether the verb is in the near future or recent past. Mark an **X** in the appropriate column.

> **Modèle**
>
> *You hear:* Pierre vient d'aller au marché.
> *You mark:* an **X** under passé récent

	passé récent	futur proche
Modèle	X	
1.		
2.		
3.		
4.		
5.		
6.		
7.		
8.		

2   **Changez** Change each sentence from the **passé composé** to the **passé récent** using the correct form of **venir de**. Repeat the correct answer after the speaker. (6 *items*)

> **Modèle**
>
> Éric et Mathilde sont allés en Corse.
> *Éric et Mathilde viennent d'aller en Corse.*

3   **Répondez** Use the **passé récent** to answer each question you hear. Repeat the correct response after the speaker. (5 *items*)

> **Modèle**
>
> Tu vas téléphoner à Martin?
> *Je viens de téléphoner à Martin.*

9A.2 The verbs devoir, vouloir, pouvoir

1 **Changez** Form a new sentence using the cue you hear as the subject. Repeat the correct answer after the speaker. (6 *items*)

> **Modèle**
>
> Je veux apprendre le français. (Mike et Sara)
> Mike et Sara veulent apprendre le français.

2 **Répondez** Answer each question you hear using the cue in your lab manual. Repeat the correct answer after the speaker.

> **Modèle**
>
> *You hear:* Est-ce que tu as pu faire tes devoirs hier soir?
> *You see:* non
> *You say:* Non, je n'ai pas pu faire mes devoirs hier soir.

1. à midi
2. des légumes
3. étudier régulièrement
4. vouloir manger des escargots
5. au marché
6. au cinéma

3 **La fête** Listen to the following description. Then read the statements in your lab manual and decide whether they are **vrai** or **faux**.

	Vrai	Faux
1. Madeleine est heureuse de pouvoir aller à l'anniversaire de Sophie.	O	O
2. Elle n'a pas voulu dire à Sophie qu'elle était fatiguée.	O	O
3. Elle a pu parler à Sophie dans l'après-midi.	O	O
4. Sophie a invité qui elle voulait.	O	O
5. Sophie et ses amis peuvent danser toute la nuit.	O	O
6. Madeleine doit organiser la musique chez Sophie.	O	O

4 **Complétez** Nathalie is at her neighbor's house. Listen to what she says and write the missing words in your lab manual.

Bonjour, excusez-moi, est-ce que (1) _____ utiliser votre téléphone, s'il vous

plaît? (2) _____ appeler un taxi immédiatement. Ma famille et moi,

(3) _____ partir tout de suite chez ma belle-mère. La situation est assez grave.

(4) _____ donner à manger à notre chat quelques jours? Mon mari et moi,

(5) _____ revenir au plus vite. Les enfants (6) _____

retourner à l'école la semaine prochaine et mon mari ne (7) _____ pas être

absent de son bureau plus d'une semaine, mais nous ne (8) _____ pas vous

donner de date précise. Si vous ne (9) _____ pas donner à manger à notre chat

tous les jours, (10) _____ aussi demander à un autre voisin de venir.

Unité 9

ESPACE CONTEXTES

Leçon 9B

1 **Logique ou illogique?** Listen to each statement and indicate whether they are **logique** or **illogique**.

	Logique	Illogique
1.	○	○
2.	○	○
3.	○	○
4.	○	○
5.	○	○
6.	○	○
7.	○	○
8.	○	○

2 **Choisissez** Listen to each statement and choose the option that completes it logically.

1. a. Il la goûte.
   b. Il la débarrasse.
2. a. Nous achetons un poivron.
   b. Nous achetons du pâté de campagne.
3. a. Le garçon la vend.
   b. Le garçon l'apporte.
4. a. avec une fourchette.
   b. avec une cuillère.
5. a. dans un verre.
   b. dans un bol.
6. a. une cuillère de sucre.
   b. une cuillère de mayonnaise.

3 **À table!** Céline has something to do tonight. Write down what it is. Then list what she has put on the table and what she has forgotten.

1. Céline doit _____

_____

2. Céline a mis _____

_____

3. Céline a oublié _____

_____

LES SONS ET LES LETTRES

Stress and rhythm

In French, all syllables are pronounced with more or less equal stress, but the final syllable in a phrase is elongated slightly.

> Je fais souvent du **sport**, mais aujourd'hui j'ai envie de rester à la mai**son**.

French sentences are divided into three basic kinds of rhythmic groups.

> *Noun phrase*   *Verb phrase*   *Prepositional phrase*
> Caroline et Dominique   sont venues   chez moi.

The final syllable of a rhythmic group may be slightly accentuated either by rising intonation (pitch) or elongation.

> Caroline et Dominique sont venues chez moi.

In English, you can add emphasis by placing more stress on certain words. In French, you can repeat the word to be emphasized by adding a pronoun or you can elongate the first consonant sound.

> Je ne sais pas, **moi**.   Quel **id**iot!   C'est **f**antastique!

---

1 **Prononcez** Répétez les phrases suivantes à voix haute.

1. Ce n'est pas vrai, ça.
2. Bonjour, Mademoiselle.
3. Moi, je m'appelle Florence.
4. La clé de ma chambre, je l'ai perdue.
5. Je voudrais un grand café noir et un croissant, s'il vous plaît.
6. Nous allons tous au marché, mais Marie, elle, va au centre commercial.

---

2 **Articulez** Répétez les phrases en mettant l'emphase sur les mots indiqués.

1. C'est *impossible*!
2. Le film était *super*!
3. Cette tarte est *délicieuse*!
4. Quelle idée *extraordinaire*!
5. Ma sœur parle *constamment*.

---

3 **Dictons** Répétez les dictons à voix haute.

1. Les chemins les plus courts ne sont pas toujours les meilleurs.
2. Le chat parti, les souris dansent.

---

4 **Dictée** You will hear six sentences. Each will be said twice. Listen carefully and write what you hear.

1. _____
2. _____
3. _____
4. _____
5. _____
6. _____

Nom _____ Date _____

9B.1 Comparatives and superlatives of adjectives and adverbs

1 **Choisissez** You will hear a series of descriptions. Choose the statement in your lab manual that expresses the correct comparison.

1. a. Simone est plus jeune que Paul. b. Simone est moins jeune que Paul.
2. a. Pierre joue moins bien que Luc. b. Pierre joue mieux que Luc.
3. a. Je regarde la télé plus souvent que toi. b. Je regarde la télé aussi souvent que toi.
4. a. Claire est plus belle qu'Odile. b. Claire est moins belle qu'Odile.
5. a. Abdel étudie plus tard que Pascal. b. Pascal étudie plus tard qu'Abdel.
6. a. Je sors aussi souvent que Julie. b. Je sors moins souvent que Julie.

2 **Comparez** Look at each drawing and answer the question you hear with a comparative statement. Repeat the correct response after the speaker.

1. Mario, Lucie   2. François, Léo   3. Alice, Joséphine

3 **Pas d'accord** Olivier and Juliette never agree. Respond to each one of Olivier's statements using the opposite comparative. Repeat the correct response after the speaker. (6 *items*)

Modèle
Malika est plus amusante que Julie.
Non, Malika *est moins amusante que Julie.*

4 **Répondez** Answer each statement you hear using the absolute superlative. Repeat the correct response after the speaker. (6 *items*)

Modèle
Les magasins sur cette avenue sont très chers.
Oui, les magasins sur cette avenue sont les plus chers.

9B.2 Double object pronouns

1 **Choisissez** Listen to each statement and choose the correct response.

1. a. Elle la lui a demandée.   b. Elle le lui a demandé.
2. a. Il la lui a apportée.   b. Il les lui a apportées.
3. a. Il le lui a décrit.   b. Il le leur a décrit.
4. a. Il vous la prépare.   b. Il vous le prépare.
5. a. Il les lui a demandées.   b. Il la lui a demandée.
6. a. Ils vont le lui laisser.   b. Ils vont les lui laisser.

2 **Changez** Repeat each statement replacing the direct and indirect object nouns with pronouns. Repeat the correct answer after the speaker. (6 *items*)

> **Modèle**
> J'ai posé la question à Michel.
> Je la lui ai *posée*.

3 **Répondez** Answer the questions using the cues you hear. Repeat the correct answer after the speaker. (6 *items*)

> **Modèle**
> Vous me servez les escargots? (non)
> Non, je ne vous les sers pas.

4 **Complétez** Magali is talking to her friend Pierre about a party. Listen to what they say and write the missing words in your lab manual.

MAGALI Jeudi prochain, c'est l'anniversaire de Jennifer et je veux lui faire une fête surprise. Elle

travaille ce jour-là, alors je (1) _____ pour samedi.

PIERRE C'est une très bonne idée. Ne t'inquiète pas, je ne vais pas (2) _____.

Si tu veux, je peux l'emmener au cinéma pendant que tu prépares la fête.

MAGALI D'accord. Julien m'a donné quelques idées pour la musique et pour les boissons. Il

(3) _____ quand nous avons parlé hier soir.

PIERRE Super! Tu as pensé au gâteau au chocolat? Je peux (4) _____. C'est

ma spécialité!

MAGALI Merci, c'est vraiment gentil. Jennifer adore le chocolat, elle va l'adorer!

PIERRE Et pour le cadeau?

MAGALI Je vais (5) _____ cet après-midi. Elle m'a parlé d'une jupe noire qu'elle

aime beaucoup dans un magasin près de chez moi. Je vais (6) _____.

PIERRE Tu as raison, le noir lui va bien.

MAGALI Bon, je pars faire mes courses. À plus tard!

PIERRE À samedi, Magali!

Unité 10

ESPACE CONTEXTES

Leçon 10A

1   **Décrivez**   For each drawing you will hear two statements. Choose the one that corresponds to it.

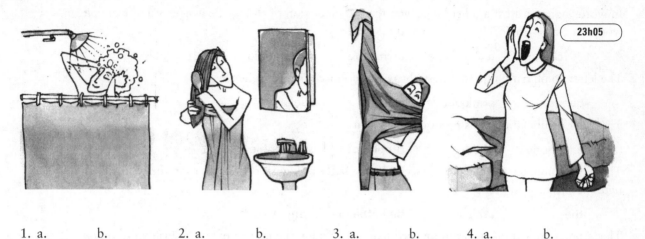

1. a.   b.   2. a.   b.   3. a.   b.   4. a.   b.

2   **Répondez**   Laure is going to baby-sit your nephew. Answer the questions about his daily routine using the cues in your lab manual. Repeat the correct response after the speaker.

> **Modèle**
>
> *You hear:* À quelle heure est-ce qu'il prend son petit-déjeuner?
> *You see:* 8h00
> *You say:* Il prend son petit-déjeuner à huit heures.

1. 7h30   3. 9h15   5. avec la serviette rouge
2. faire sa toilette   4. non   6. après tous les repas

3   **La routine de Frédéric**   Listen to Frédéric talk about his daily routine. Then read the statements in your lab manual and decide whether they are vrai or faux.

	Vrai	Faux
1. Frédéric se réveille tous les matins à six heures.	O	O
2. Frédéric va acheter une baguette à la boulangerie.	O	O
3. Frédéric prépare le café.	O	O
4. Frédéric se maquille.	O	O
5. Frédéric se lave et se rase.	O	O
6. Frédéric s'habille lentement.	O	O
7. Frédéric ne se brosse jamais les dents.	O	O

LES SONS ET LES LETTRES

ch, qu, ph, th, and gn

The letter combination **ch** is usually pronounced like the English *sh*, as in the word *shoe*.

    chat   **ch**ien   **ch**ose   en**ch**anté

In words borrowed from other languages, the pronunciation of **ch** may be irregular. For example, in words of Greek origin, **ch** is pronounced **k**.

    psy**ch**ologie   te**ch**nologie   ar**ch**aïque   ar**ch**éologie

The letter combination **qu** is almost always pronounced like the letter **k**.

    quand   prati**qu**er   kios**qu**e   **qu**elle

The letter combination **ph** is pronounced like an **f**.

    télé**ph**one   **ph**oto   pro**ph**ète   géogra**ph**ie

The letter combination **th** is pronounced like the letter **t**. English *th* sounds, as in the words *this* and *with*, never occur in French.

    thé   a**th**lète   biblio**th**èque   sympa**th**ique

The letter combination **gn** is pronounced like the sound in the middle of the English word *onion*.

    monta**gn**e   espa**gn**ol   ga**gn**er   Allema**gn**e

1   **Prononcez** Répétez les mots suivants à voix haute.

    1. thé   4. question   7. champagne   10. fréquenter
    2. quart   5. cheveux   8. casquette   11. photographie
    3. chose   6. parce que   9. philosophie   12. sympathique

2   **Articulez** Répétez les phrases suivantes à voix haute.

    1. Quentin est martiniquais ou québécois?
    2. Quelqu'un explique la question à Joseph.
    3. Pourquoi est-ce que Philippe est inquiet?
    4. Ignace prend une photo de la montagne.
    5. Monique fréquente un café en Belgique.
    6. Théo étudie la physique.

3   **Dictons** Répétez les dictons à voix haute.

    1. La vache la première au pré lèche la rosée.   2. N'éveillez pas le chat qui dort.

4   **Dictée** You will hear six sentences. Each will be said twice. Listen carefully and write what you hear.

    1. _____
    2. _____
    3. _____
    4. _____
    5. _____
    6. _____

ESPACE STRUCTURES

10A.1 Reflexive verbs

1 **Transformez** Form a new sentence using the cue you hear. Repeat the correct answer after the speaker. (6 items)

> **Modèle**
> Je me lève à huit heures. (mon frère)
> **Mon frère se lève à huit heures.**

2 **Répondez** Answer each question you hear using the cues in your lab manual. Repeat the correct response after the speaker.

> **Modèle**
> _You hear:_ Tu prends un bain tous les matins?
> _You see:_ non
> _You say:_ **Non, je ne prends pas de bain tous les matins.**

1. tôt
2. le matin
3. oui / nous
4. non
5. non
6. après minuit

3 **Qu'est-ce qu'il dit?** Listen to Gérard talk about his family. Replace what he says with a reflexive verb. Repeat the correct response after the speaker. (6 items)

> **Modèle**
> Je sors de mon lit.
> _Je me lève._

4 **En vacances** Answer each question you hear with a command using the cue you hear. Repeat the correct response after the speaker. (8 items)

> **Modèle**
> Je prends un bain? (non)
> _Non, ne prends pas de bain._

10A.2 Reflexives: **Sens idiomatique**

1 **Décrivez** For each drawing you will hear two statements. Choose the one that corresponds to the drawing.

1. a.   b.   2. a.   b.   3. a.   b.   4. a.   b.

2 **Répondez** Answer each question you hear in the affirmative. Repeat the correct response after the speaker. (6 *items*)

> **Modèle**
>
> Est-ce que tu t'entends bien avec ta sœur?
> *Oui, je m'entends bien avec ma sœur.*

3 **Les deux sœurs** Listen as Amélie describes her relationship with her sister. Then read the statements in your lab manual and decide whether they are vrai or faux.

	Vrai	Faux
1. Amélie et Joëlle s'entendent bien.	○	○
2. Elles s'intéressent à la politique.	○	○
3. Elles ne se disputent jamais.	○	○
4. Quand elles sont ensemble, elles s'ennuient parfois.	○	○
5. Amélie est étudiante et Joëlle travaille.	○	○
6. Joëlle s'habille très bien.	○	○
7. Le samedi, elles se reposent dans un parc du centre-ville.	○	○
8. Elles s'énervent quand elles essaient des robes et des tee-shirts.	○	○

Unité 10

Leçon 10B

ESPACE CONTEXTES

1 **Décrivez** For each drawing you will hear two statements. Choose the one that corresponds to the drawing.

1. a.   b.

2. a.   b.

3. a.   b.

4. a.   b.

2 **Identifiez** You will hear a series of words. Write each one in the appropriate category.

> **Modèle**
>
> *You hear:* Il tousse.
> *You write:* **tousse** under **symptôme**

	endroit	symptôme	diagnostic	traitement
Modèle	_____	tousse	_____	_____
1.	_____	_____	_____	_____
2.	_____	_____	_____	_____
3.	_____	_____	_____	_____
4.	_____	_____	_____	_____
5.	_____	_____	_____	_____
6.	_____	_____	_____	_____
7.	_____	_____	_____	_____
8.	_____	_____	_____	_____
9.	_____	_____	_____	_____
10.	_____	_____	_____	_____

LES SONS ET LES LETTRES

p, t, and c

Read the following English words aloud while holding your hand an inch or two in front of your mouth. You should feel a small burst of air when you pronounce each of the consonants.

  pan   **top**   **cope**   **pat**

In French, the letters **p**, **t**, and **c** are not accompanied by a short burst of air. This time, try to minimize the amount of air you exhale as you pronounce these consonants. You should feel only a very small burst of air or none at all.

  panne   **taupe**   **capital**   **cœur**

To minimize a **t** sound, touch your tongue to your teeth and gums, rather than just your gums.

  taille   **tête**   **tomber**   **tousser**

Similarly, you can minimize the force of a **p** by smiling slightly as you pronounce it.

  pied   **poitrine**   **pilule**   **piqûre**

When you pronounce a hard **k** sound, you can minimize the force by releasing it very quickly.

  corps   **cou**   **casser**   **comme**

---

1   **Prononcez** Répétez les mots suivants à voix haute.

1. plat	4. timide	7. pardon	10. problème	13. petits pois
2. cave	5. commencer	8. carotte	11. rencontrer	14. colocataire
3. tort	6. travailler	9. partager	12. confiture	15. canadien

---

2   **Articulez** Répétez les phrases suivantes à voix haute.

1. Paul préfère le tennis ou les cartes?   3. Claire et Thomas ont-ils la grippe?
2. Claude déteste le poisson et le café.   4. Tu préfères les biscuits ou les gâteaux?

---

3   **Dictons** Répétez les dictons à voix haute.

1. Les absents ont toujours tort.
2. Il n'y a que le premier pas qui coûte.

---

4   **Dictée** You will hear six sentences. Each will be said twice. Listen carefully and write what you hear.

1. _____
2. _____
3. _____
4. _____
5. _____
6. _____

ESPACE STRUCTURES

10B.1 The passé composé of reflexive verbs

1 **Identifiez** Listen to each sentence and decide whether the verb is in the présent, imparfait, or passé composé.

Modèle

You hear: Michel a mal aux dents.
You mark: an **X** under **présent**

	présent	imparfait	passé composé
Modèle	X		
1.			
2.			
3.			
4.			
5.			
6.			
7.			
8.			
9.			
10.			

2 **Changez** Change each sentence from the **présent** to the **passé composé**. Repeat the correct answer after the speaker. (*8 items*)

Modèle

Nous nous reposons après le tennis.
Nous nous sommes reposés après le tennis.

3 **Répondez** Answer each question you hear using the cue in your lab manual. Repeat the correct response after the speaker.

Modèle

You hear: Est-ce que tu t'es ennuyé au concert?
You see: non
You say: Non, je ne me suis pas ennuyé au concert.

1. se promener   2. se tromper d'adresse   3. non   4. tôt   5. bien sûr   6. oui

4 **Complétez** Listen to Véronique's story and write the missing words in your lab manual.

Manon (1) _____ quand Véronique, sa fille de onze ans, n'est pas rentrée de l'école à

cinq heures. Elle (2) _____ de lire et a regardé par la fenêtre. À cinq heures et demie, elle

(3) _____. Dans la rue, à six heures, Véronique (4) _____ de rentrer. Qu'est-il arrivé

à Véronique? Elle est sortie de l'école avec une amie; elles (5) _____ et elles (6) _____

dans une boulangerie. Véronique a ensuite quitté son amie, mais elle (7) _____ de rue. Quand

Véronique est finalement rentrée à la maison, Manon (8) _____. Véronique (9) _____

que sa mère avait eu peur et elles ont rapidement arrêté de (10) _____.

10B.2 The pronouns y and en

1 Choisissez Listen to each question and choose the most logical answer.

1. a. Non, je n'en ai pas.   b. Non, je n'y ai pas.
2. a. Oui, nous les faisons.   b. Oui, nous en faisons.
3. a. Oui, il en fait régulièrement. b. Oui, il y va régulièrement.
4. a. Non, nous en prenons pas souvent. b. Non, nous n'en prenons pas souvent.
5. a. Oui, ils n'y sont pas allés.   b. Oui, ils y sont allés.
6. a. Non, je ne vais pas en boire.   b. Non, je n'en bois pas.
7. a. Oui, nous y allons.   b. Oui, nous en allons.
8. a. Oui, nous y revenons.   b. Oui, nous en revenons.

2 Changez Restate each sentence you hear using the pronouns y or en. Repeat the correct answer after the speaker. (*8 items*)

> **Modèle**
>
> Nous sommes allés chez le dentiste.
> Nous y sommes allés.

3 Répondez André is at his doctor's for a check-up. Answer each question using the cues you hear. Repeat the correct answer after the speaker. (*6 items*)

> **Modèle**
>
> Vous habitez à Lyon? (oui)
> Oui, j'y habite.

4 Aux urgences Listen to the dialogue between the nurse, Madame Pinon, and her daughter Florence, and write the missing answers in your lab manual.

1. **INFIRMIÈRE** C'est la première fois que vous venez aux urgences?

2. **MME PINON** _____

3. **INFIRMIÈRE** Vous avez un médecin?

4. **MME PINON** _____

5. **INFIRMIÈRE** Vous avez une allergie, Mademoiselle?

6. **FLORENCE** _____

7. **MME PINON** Vous allez lui faire une piqûre?

8. **INFIRMIÈRE** _____

Unité 11

ESPACE CONTEXTES

1   **Associez**   Circle the word or words that are logically associated with each word you hear.

1. imprimante	CD	écran
2. clavier	page d'accueil	être connecté
3. enregistrer	éteindre	sonner
4. téléphone	baladeur CD	portable
5. démarrer	fermer	sauvegarder
6. télévision	stéréo	jeu vidéo

2   **Logique ou illogique?**   Listen to these statements and indicate whether each one is **logique** or **illogique**.

	Logique	Illogique
1.	○	○
2.	○	○
3.	○	○
4.	○	○
5.	○	○
6.	○	○
7.	○	○
8.	○	○

3   **Décrivez**   For each drawing, you will hear three statements. Choose the one that corresponds to the drawing.

1. a.   b.   c.   2. a.   b.   c.

Nom _____   Date _____

Final consonants

You already learned that final consonants are usually silent, except for the letters **c**, **r**, **f**, and **l**.

     ave**c**   hive**r**   che**f**   hôte**l**

You've probably noticed other exceptions to this rule. Often, such exceptions are words borrowed from other languages. These final consonants are pronounced.

   Latin   *English*   *Inuit*   *Latin*
   foru**m**   sno**b**   anora**k**   ga**z**

Numbers, geographical directions, and proper names are common exceptions.

   cin**q**   su**d**   Agnè**s**   Maghre**b**

Some words with identical spellings are pronounced differently to distinguish between meanings or parts of speech.

   fil**s** = *son*   fil~~s~~ = *threads*
   tou**s** (pronoun) = *everyone*   tou~~s~~ (adjective) = *all*

The word **plus** can have three different pronunciations.

   plu~~s~~ de (silent s)   plu**s** que (s sound)   plus‿ou moins (z sound in liaison)

1   **Prononcez** Répétez les mots suivants à voix haute.

1. cap
2. six
3. truc
4. club
5. slip
6. actif
7. strict
8. avril
9. index
10. Alfred
11. bifteck
12. bus

2   **Articulez** Répétez les phrases suivantes à voix haute.

1. Leur fils est gentil, mais il est très snob.
2. Au restaurant, nous avons tous pris du bifteck.
3. Le sept août, David assiste au forum sur le Maghreb.
4. Alex et Ludovic jouent au tennis dans un club de sport.
5. Prosper prend le bus pour aller à l'est de la ville.

3   **Dictons** Répétez les dictons à voix haute.

1. Plus on boit, plus on a soif.   2. Un pour tous, tous pour un!

4   **Dictée** You will hear eight sentences. Each will be read twice. Listen carefully and write what you hear.

1. _____
2. _____
3. _____
4. _____
5. _____
6. _____
7. _____
8. _____

ESPACE STRUCTURES

11A.1 Prepositions with the infinitive

1 **Identifiez** Listen to each statement and mark an **X** in the column of the preposition you hear before the infinitive.

> **Modèle**
>
> _You hear:_ Yasmina n'a pas pensé à acheter des fleurs.
> _You mark:_ an **X** under **à**

	à	de	pas de préposition
Modèle	X	_____	_____
1.	_____	_____	_____
2.	_____	_____	_____
3.	_____	_____	_____
4.	_____	_____	_____
5.	_____	_____	_____
6.	_____	_____	_____
7.	_____	_____	_____
8.	_____	_____	_____

2 **Choisissez** You will hear some statements with a beep in place of the preposition. Decide which preposition should complete each sentence.

	à	de		à	de
1.	○	○	5.	○	○
2.	○	○	6.	○	○
3.	○	○	7.	○	○
4.	○	○	8.	○	○

3 **Questions** Answer each question you hear in the affirmative, using the cue in your lab manual. Repeat the correct response after the speaker.

> **Modèle**
>
> _You hear:_ Tu as réussi?
> _You see:_ fermer le logiciel
> _You say:_ Oui, j'ai réussi à fermer le logiciel.

1. télécharger le document
2. enregistrer
3. utiliser le caméscope
4. se connecter
5. éteindre le magnétoscope
6. imprimer des photos
7. surfer jusqu'à 11 heures
8. partir tout de suite

4 **Finissez** You will hear incomplete sentences. Choose the correct ending for each sentence.

1. a. à sauvegarder mon document.
   b. de trouver la solution.
2. a. d'acheter un nouveau logiciel.
   b. éteindre l'ordinateur.
3. a. à sortir le soir.
   b. de regarder la télé.
4. a. acheter un caméscope ce week-end.
   b. à trouver un appareil photo pas trop cher.
5. a. de fermer la fenêtre.
   b. éteindre le moniteur.
6. a. d'essayer un nouveau jeu vidéo?
   b. à nettoyer son bureau?

11A.2 Reciprocal reflexives

1 **Questions** Answer each question you hear in the negative. Repeat the correct response after the speaker. (6 _items_)

> **Modèle**
>
> Est-ce que vous vous êtes rencontrés ici?
> _Non, nous ne nous sommes pas rencontrés ici._

2 **Conjuguez** Form a new sentence using the cue you hear as the subject. Repeat the correct answer after the speaker. (6 _items_)

> **Modèle**
>
> Marion s'entend bien avec sa famille. (vous)
> _Vous vous entendez bien avec votre famille._

3 **Identifiez** Listen to Clara describe her relationship with her friend Anne. Listen to each sentence and write the infinitive(s) of the verb(s) you hear.

1. _____   5. _____

2. _____   6. _____

3. _____   7. _____

4. _____   8. _____

4 **Les rencontres** Listen to each statement and write the number of the statement below the drawing it describes. There are more statements than there are drawings.

a. _____   b. _____   c. _____

d. _____   e. _____

Unité 11

ESPACE CONTEXTES

Leçon 11B

1 **Logique ou illogique?** Listen to these statements and indicate whether each one is **logique** or **illogique**.

	Logique	Illogique			Logique	Illogique
1.	○	○		5.	○	○
2.	○	○		6.	○	○
3.	○	○		7.	○	○
4.	○	○		8.	○	○

2 **Les problèmes** Listen to people complaining about problems with their car and decide whether they need to take their car to the garage to get repaired or not.

> **Modèle**
>
> *You hear:* Mon embrayage est cassé.
> *You mark:* an **X** under **Visite chez le mécanicien nécessaire**

	Visite chez le mécanicien nécessaire	Visite pas nécessaire
Modèle	X	
1.	_____	_____
2.	_____	_____
3.	_____	_____
4.	_____	_____
5.	_____	_____
6.	_____	_____
7.	_____	_____
8.	_____	_____

3 **Décrivez** For each drawing, you will hear three brief descriptions. Indicate whether they are **vrai** or **faux** according to what you see.

1. a. vrai   a. faux
   b. vrai   b. faux
   c. vrai   c. faux

2. a. vrai   a. faux
   b. vrai   b. faux
   c. vrai   c. faux

1.

2.

LES SONS ET LES LETTRES

The letter x

The letter **x** in French is sometimes pronounced *-ks*, like the *x* in the English word *axe*.

taxi   ex**pl**iquer   me**x**icain   te**x**te

Unlike English, some French words begin with a *gz-* sound.

xylophone   **x**énon   **x**énophile   **X**avière

The letters **ex-** followed by a vowel are often pronounced like the English word *eggs*.

exemple   **exa**men   **exi**l   **exa**ct

Sometimes an **x** is pronounced *s*, as in the following numbers.

soi**x**ante   si**x**   di**x**

An **x** is pronounced *z* in a liaison. Otherwise, an **x** at the end of a word is usually silent.

deu**x** enfants   si**x** éléphants   mieu**x̸**   curieu**x̸**

---

1 **Prononcez** Répétez les mots suivants à voix haute.

1. fax
2. eux
3. dix
4. prix
5. jeux
6. index
7. excuser
8. exercice
9. orageux
10. expression
11. contexte
12. sérieux

---

2 **Articulez** Répétez les phrases suivantes à voix haute.

1. Les amoureux sont devenus époux.
2. Soixante-dix euros! La note (*bill*) du taxi est exorbitante!
3. Alexandre est nerveux parce qu'il a deux examens.
4. Xavier explore le vieux quartier d'Aix-en-Provence.
5. Le professeur explique l'exercice aux étudiants exceptionnels.

---

3 **Dictons** Répétez les dictons à voix haute.

1. Les beaux esprits se rencontrent.
2. Les belles plumes font les beaux oiseaux.

---

4 **Dictée** You will hear eight sentences. Each will be read twice. Listen carefully and write what you hear.

1. _____
2. _____
3. _____
4. _____
5. _____
6. _____
7. _____
8. _____

ESPACE STRUCTURES

11B.1 The verbs **ouvrir** and **offrir**

1 **Identifiez** Listen to each sentence and write the infinitive of the verb you hear.

> **Modèle**
> *You hear:* J'offre rarement des fleurs à mes enfants.
> *You write:* offrir

1. _____   5. _____

2. _____   6. _____

3. _____   7. _____

4. _____   8. _____

2 **Conjuguez** Form a new sentence using the cue you hear as the subject. Repeat the correct answer after the speaker. (*6 items*)

> **Modèle**
> Il ouvre le magasin tous les matins. (nous)
> **Nous ouvrons le magasin tous les matins.**

3 **Questions** Answer each question you hear using the cue in your lab manual. Repeat the correct response after the speaker.

> **Modèle**
> *You hear:* Comment tu as ouvert ce fichier?
> *You see:* mot de passe
> *You say:* J'ai ouvert ce fichier avec un mot de passe.

1. un nouvel ordinateur   4. rarement
2. il y a deux jours   5. un voyage au Maroc
3. le soir   6. de cuir (*leather*)

4 **Décrivez** For each drawing, you will hear two statements. Choose the one that corresponds to the drawing.

1.    2.

3.    4.

1. a.   b.

2. a.   b.

3. a.   b.

4. a.   b.

Unité 11 Lab Activities   **87**

11B.2 Le conditionnel

1 **Choisissez** Listen to each sentence and decide whether you hear a verb in the indicative or the conditional.

1. indicatif   conditionnel
2. indicatif   conditionnel
3. indicatif   conditionnel
4. indicatif   conditionnel
5. indicatif   conditionnel
6. indicatif   conditionnel
7. indicatif   conditionnel
8. indicatif   conditionnel

2 **Identifiez** Listen to each sentence and write the infinitive of the conjugated verb you hear.

> **Modèle**
>
> *You hear:* Nous pourrions prendre l'autre voiture.
> *You write: pouvoir*

1. _____   4. _____

2. _____   5. _____

3. _____   6. _____

3 **Complétez** Form a new sentence using the cue you hear as the subject. Repeat the correct response after the speaker. (6 *items*)

> **Modèle**
>
> Je vérifierais la pression des pneus. (le mécanicien).
> *Le mécanicien vérifierait la pression des pneus.*

4 **Identifiez** Listen to Ophélie talk about what her life would be like if she had a car. Write the missing verbs.

Je (1) _____ une voiture à tout prix (*at any price*)! Si j'avais une voiture, je

(2) _____ travailler loin de la maison. Je n' (3) _____

pas besoin de prendre le train et le bus. Mes amis et moi (4) _____ souvent en

voiture au centre-ville pour faire du shopping ou voir des films. Et on (5) _____

ensemble au restaurant de temps en temps. Ce (6) _____ trop bien! Et puis, le

soir, on (7) _____ à la maison très tard en sécurité (*safely*). Mais avant d'acheter

une voiture, je (8) _____ avoir mon permis de conduire!

Unité 12

Leçon 12A

ESPACE CONTEXTES

1 **Logique ou illogique?** Listen to these sentences and indicate whether each one is **logique** or **illogique**.

	Logique	Illogique
1.	○	○
2.	○	○
3.	○	○
4.	○	○
5.	○	○
6.	○	○
7.	○	○
8.	○	○

2 **Les courses** Look at the drawing in your lab manual and listen to Rachel's description of her day. During each pause, write the name of the place she went. The first one has been done for you.

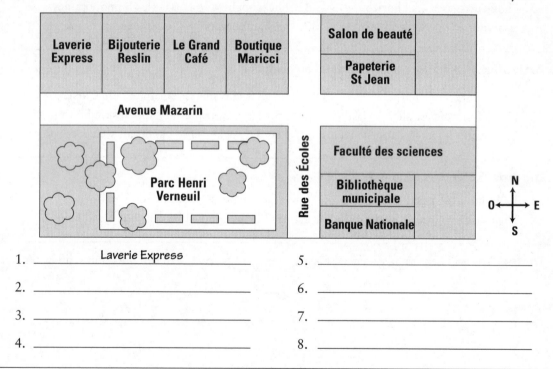

1. ___Laverie Express___   5. _____

2. _____   6. _____

3. _____   7. _____

4. _____   8. _____

3 **Questions** Look once again at the drawing in **Activité 2** in your lab manual and answer each question you hear with the correct information. Repeat the correct response after the speaker. (*6 items*)

> **Modèle**
>
> Il y a une laverie rue des Écoles?
> Non, il y a une laverie avenue Mazarin.

LES SONS ET LES LETTRES

The letter h

You already know that the letter **h** is silent in French, and you are familiar with many French words that begin with an **h muet**. In such words, the letter **h** is treated as if it were a vowel. For example, the articles **le** and **la** become **l'** and there is a liaison between the final consonant of a preceding word and the vowel following the **h**.

l'heure   l'homme   des hôtels   des hommes

Some words begin with an **h aspiré**. In such words, the **h** is still silent, but it is not treated like a vowel. Words beginning with **h aspiré**, like these you've already learned, are not preceded by **l'** and there is no liaison.

la honte   les haricots verts   le huit mars   les hors-d'œuvre

Words that begin with an **h aspiré** are normally indicated in dictionaries by some kind of symbol, usually an asterisk (*).

1 **Prononcez** Répétez les mots suivants à voix haute.

1. le hall
2. la hi-fi
3. l'humeur
4. la honte
5. le héron
6. l'horloge
7. l'horizon
8. le hippie
9. l'hilarité
10. la Hongrie
11. l'hélicoptère
12. les hamburgers
13. les hiéroglyphes
14. les hors-d'œuvre
15. les hippopotames
16. l'hiver

2 **Articulez** Répétez les phrases suivantes à voix haute.

1. Hélène joue de la harpe.
2. Hier, Honorine est allée à l'hôpital.
3. Le hamster d'Hervé s'appelle Henri.
4. La Havane est la capitale de Cuba.
5. L'anniversaire d'Héloïse est le huit mars.
6. Le hockey et le hand-ball sont mes sports préférés.

3 **Dictons** Répétez les dictons à voix haute.

1. La honte n'est pas d'être inférieur à l'adversaire, c'est d'être inférieur à soi-même.
2. L'heure, c'est l'heure; avant l'heure, c'est pas l'heure; après l'heure, c'est plus l'heure.

4 **Dictée** You will hear eight sentences. Each will be read twice. Listen carefully and write what you hear.

1. _____
2. _____
3. _____
4. _____
5. _____
6. _____
7. _____
8. _____

ESPACE STRUCTURES

12A.1 Voir, recevoir, apercevoir, and croire

1 **Choisissez** You will hear some sentences with a beep in place of the verb. Circle the form of **voir**, **recevoir**, **apercevoir**, or **croire** that correctly completes each sentence.

> **Modèle**
> *You hear:* Jeanne *(beep)* Guillaume à la banque.
> *You see:* aperçoit   avons aperçu
> *You circle:* aperçoit

1. aperçois   avez aperçu
2. ont reçu   recevons
3. reçoivent   reçoit
4. apercevons   aperçoit
5. croit   as cru
6. voient   voit

2 **Conjuguez** Form a new sentence using the cue you hear as the subject. Repeat the correct answer after the speaker.

> **Modèle**
> Vous ne recevez pas cette chaîne ici.
> (Monsieur David)
> **Monsieur David ne reçoit pas cette chaîne ici.**

1. (nous)   3. (tu)   5. (il)
2. (elles)   4. (je)   6. (vous)

3 **Questions** Answer each question you hear using the cue in your lab manual. Repeat the correct response after the speaker.

> **Modèle**
> *You hear:* Où est-ce qu'il a aperçu la poste?
> *You see:* en face
> *You say:* Il a aperçu la poste en face.

1. le 19   4. la semaine dernière
2. à la poste   5. devant la banque
3. le mois de janvier   6. oui

4 **La liste** Look at Hervé's shopping list for Christmas and answer each question you hear. Repeat the correct response after the speaker. *(6 items)*

Aurore	un rendez-vous dans un salon de beauté
grands-parents	un voyage à la Martinique
cousin François	du papier à lettres
parents	un lecteur de DVD et un caméscope
Jean-Michel	une montre

Unité 12 Lab Activities

12A.2 Negative/Affirmative expressions

1 **Identifiez** Listen to each statement and mark an **X** in the column of the negative expression you hear.

> **Modèle**
>
> *You hear:* Je ne reçois jamais de lettre.
> *You mark:* an **X** under **ne... jamais**

	ne... rien	ne... que	personne	ne... personne	ne... jamais	ne... plus
Modèle	_____	_____	_____	_____	X	_____
1.	_____	_____	_____	_____	_____	_____
2.	_____	_____	_____	_____	_____	_____
3.	_____	_____	_____	_____	_____	_____
4.	_____	_____	_____	_____	_____	_____
5.	_____	_____	_____	_____	_____	_____
6.	_____	_____	_____	_____	_____	_____
7.	_____	_____	_____	_____	_____	_____
8.	_____	_____	_____	_____	_____	_____

2 **Transformez** Change each sentence you hear to say the opposite is true. Repeat the correct answer after the speaker. (*6 items*)

> **Modèle**
>
> Je vais toujours à cette agence.
> *Je ne vais jamais à cette agence.*

3 **Questions** Answer each question you hear in the negative. Repeat the correct response after the speaker. (*6 items*)

> **Modèle**
>
> Vous avez reçu quelqu'un aujourd'hui?
> *Non, nous n'avons reçu personne.*

4 **Au téléphone** Listen to this phone conversation between Philippe and Sophie. Then decide whether the statements in your lab manual are **vrai** or **faux.**

	Vrai	Faux
1. Philippe ne peut voir personne aujourd'hui.	○	○
2. Il n'a jamais organisé de rendez-vous.	○	○
3. Le service de Sophie n'a rien reçu.	○	○
4. Il n'y a aucun rendez-vous pour le lundi matin.	○	○
5. Il ne reste de rendez-vous que pour le lundi matin.	○	○

Unité 12

Leçon 12B

1 **Orientez-vous** Listen to each pair of places and describe their location in relation to each other using the cue in your lab manual. Repeat the correct answer after the speaker.

> **Modèle**
> *You hear:* Paris, New York
> *You see:* est
> *You say:* Paris est à l'est de New York.

1. nord   3. près de   5. ouest
2. est   4. loin de   6. sud

2 **Décrivez** Look at the drawing and listen to each statement. Indicate whether each statement is **vrai** or **faux**.

	Vrai	Faux
1.	○	○
2.	○	○
3.	○	○
4.	○	○
5.	○	○
6.	○	○

3 **Complétez** Listen to Laurent describe where he lives and write the missing words in your lab manual.

Voici les (1) _____ pour venir chez moi. À la sortie de l'aéroport, suivez le

(2) _____ jusqu'au centre-ville. Quand vous arrivez à la fontaine,

(3) _____ à droite. Prenez le (4) _____ pour

(5) _____ Tournez ensuite dans la première rue à droite et

(6) _____ (7) _____ jusqu'au bout de la rue. J'habite un

grand (8) _____ à l'angle de cette rue et de l'avenue Saint-Michel.

LES SONS ET LES LETTRES

Les majuscules et les minuscules

Some of the rules governing capitalization are the same in French as they are in English. However, many words that are capitalized in English are not capitalized in French. For example, the French pronoun **je** is never capitalized except when it is the first word in a sentence.

Aujourd'hui, **je** vais au marché.   *Today, I am going to the market.*

Days of the week, months, and geographical terms are not capitalized in French.

Qu'est-ce que tu fais **l**undi après-midi?   Mon anniversaire, c'est le 14 **o**ctobre.
Cette ville est au bord de la **m**er Méditerranée.

Languages are not capitalized in French, nor are adjectives of nationality. However, if the word is a noun that refers to a person or people of a particular nationality, it is capitalized.

Tu apprends le français.   C'est une voiture allemande.
You are learning French.   *It's a German car.*

Elle s'est mariée avec un Italien.   Les Français adorent le foot.
She married an Italian.   *The French love soccer.*

As a general rule, you should write capital letters with their accents. Diacritical marks can change the meaning of words, so not including them can create ambiguities.

LES AVOCATS SERONT JUG**É**S.   LES AVOCATS SERONT JUGES.
Lawyers will be judged.   *Lawyers will be the judges.*

---

1 **Décidez** Listen to these sentences and decide whether the words below should be capitalized.

1. a. canadienne   b. Canadienne   5. a. océan   b. Océan
2. a. avril   b. Avril   6. a. je   b. Je
3. a. japonais   b. Japonais   7. a. mercredi   b. Mercredi
4. a. québécoises   b. Québécoises   8. a. marocain   b. Marocain

---

2 **Écoutez** You will hear a paragraph containing the words in the list. Check the appropriate column to indicate whether they should be capitalized.

	Majuscule	Minuscule			Majuscule	Minuscule
1. lundi	_____	_____		4. suisse	_____	_____
2. avenue	_____	_____		5. quartier	_____	_____
3. français	_____	_____				

---

3 **Dictée** You will hear eight sentences. Each will be read twice. Listen carefully and write what you hear.

1. _____
2. _____
3. _____
4. _____
5. _____
6. _____
7. _____
8. _____

12B.1 Le futur simple

1 Identifiez Listen to each sentence and write the infinitive of the verb you hear.

> **Modèle**
>
> *You hear:* Ils se déplaceront pour le 14 juillet.
> *You write: se déplacer*

1. _____   5. _____

2. _____   6. _____

3. _____   7. _____

4. _____   8. _____

2 Transformez Change each sentence from the present to the future. Repeat the correct answer after the speaker.

> **Modèle**
>
> Bertrand travaille près d'ici. (Bertrand)
> *Bertrand travaillera près d'ici.*

1. (je)   3. (la mairie)   5. (on)   7. (Malik)
2. (vous)   4. (vous)   6. (nous)   8. (ils)

3 Questions Answer each question you hear using the cue in your lab manual. Repeat the correct response after the speaker.

> **Modèle**
>
> *You hear:* Quand est-ce que tu retrouveras
>   ta cousine?
> *You see:* jeudi
> *You say: Je retrouverai ma cousine jeudi.*

1. 8 heures et demie   4. Jean-Pierre et son équipe
2. nous   5. en train
3. sur la droite   6. au carrefour

4 Le futur Look at the timeline, which shows future events in Christian's life, and answer each question you hear. Then repeat the correct response after the speaker. (*6 items*)

Unité 12 Lab Activities   **95**

12B.2 Irregular future forms

1 **Identifiez** Listen to each statement and mark an **X** in the column of the verb you hear.

> _You hear:_ Nous ne serons pas au parc cet après-midi.
> _You mark:_ an **X** under **être**

	aller	avoir	être	faire	savoir
Modèle	_____	_____	X	_____	_____
1.	_____	_____	_____	_____	_____
2.	_____	_____	_____	_____	_____
3.	_____	_____	_____	_____	_____
4.	_____	_____	_____	_____	_____
5.	_____	_____	_____	_____	_____
6.	_____	_____	_____	_____	_____
7.	_____	_____	_____	_____	_____
8.	_____	_____	_____	_____	_____

2 **Choisissez** Listen to each question and choose the most logical response.

1. a. Non, nous ne viendrons pas.   b. Non, nous irons samedi.
2. a. Oui, ils l'apercevront de la fenêtre.   b. Oui, ils viendront au parc.
3. a. Non, elle tournera.   b. Oui, vous continuerez vers la droite.
4. a. Oui, je te montrerai.   b. Non, tu ne voudras pas.
5. a. Non, il les enverra à temps.   b. Oui, il les aura à temps.
6. a. Oui, elle ira en mars.   b. Non, ses cousins seront là pour l'aider.
7. a. Oui, il pourra la poster au bout de la rue.   b. Oui, il l'écrira.
8. a. Tu ne le feras jamais.   b. Tu pourras visiter le musée.

3 **Décrivez** For each drawing, you will hear two statements. Choose the one that corresponds to the drawing.

1. a.   b.   2. a.   b.   3. a.   b.

4. a.   b.   5. a.   b.   6. a.   b.

4 **En ville** Listen to Brigitte and Zoé talk about their plans for tomorrow. Then read the statements in your lab manual and decide whether they are **vrai** or **faux**.

	Vrai	Faux
1. Zoé n'ira pas en ville demain.	○	○
2. Elle fera des courses l'après-midi.	○	○
3. Elle viendra chercher Brigitte à son travail.	○	○
4. Brigitte aura ses photos.	○	○
5. Zoé verra le bureau de Brigitte.	○	○
6. Ça sera sympa.	○	○

Unité 13

ESPACE CONTEXTES

1   **Identifiez** You will hear a series of words. Write the word that does not belong in each series.

1. _____   5. _____

2. _____   6. _____

3. _____   7. _____

4. _____   8. _____

2   **Logique ou illogique?** Listen to these statements and indicate whether they are **logique** or **illogique**.

	Logique	Illogique		Logique	Illogique
1.	○	○	5.	○	○
2.	○	○	6.	○	○
3.	○	○	7.	○	○
4.	○	○	8.	○	○

3   **Les annonces** Look at the ads and listen to each statement. Then decide if the statement is **vrai** or **faux**.

SPÉCIALISTES BEAUTÉ

Recherchons 5 spécialistes "beauté-forme" sur Paris.

- 3 ans d'expérience minimum
- excellente présentation
- bon contact avec les client(e)s
- sérieux et professionnalisme

Envoyez lettre de motivation et C.V à Mme Fréchine, Salon de beauté Sublime, 58 avenue de Constantinople, 75008 Paris.

VENDEURS/VENDEUSES

- Compagnie de production d'une boisson aux fruits célèbre recherche des vendeurs/vendeuses dans toute la France.
- De formation commerciale supérieure (Bac + 2 minimum), vous avez déjà une solide expérience. (5 ans minimum)
- Salaire: 3800 euros par mois.

Pour plus d'information, rendez-vous sur le site http://www.boissonauxfruitssympa.com

	Vrai	Faux
1.	○	○
2.	○	○
3.	○	○
4.	○	○
5.	○	○
6.	○	○

La ponctuation française

Although French uses most of the same punctuation marks as English, their usage often varies. Unlike English, no period (**point**) is used in abbreviations of measurements in French.

> 200 **m** *(meters)*   30 **min** *(minutes)*   25 **cl** *(centiliters)*   500 **g** *(grams)*

In other abbreviations, a period is used only if the last letter of the abbreviation is different from the last letter of the word they represent.

> **Mme** Bonaire = Mada**me** Bonaire   **M.** Bonaire = Monsieu**r** Bonaire

French dates are written with the day before the month, so if the month is spelled out, no punctuation is needed. When using digits only, use slashes to separate them.

> le 25 février 1954   25/2/1954   le 15 août 2006   15/8/2006

Notice that a comma (**une virgule**) is not used before the last item in a series or list.

> Lucie parle français, anglais et allemand.   *Lucie speaks French, English, and German.*

Generally, in French, a direct quotation is enclosed in **guillemets**. Notice that a colon (**deux points**), not a comma, is used before the quotation.

> Charlotte a dit: «Appelle-moi!»   Marc a demandé: «Qui est à l'appareil?»

1 La ponctuation Repeat the names of these punctuation marks in French.

1. un point (.)
2. une virgule (,)
3. un trait d'union (-)
4. un point d'interrogation (?)
5. un point d'exclamation (!)
6. deux points (:)
7. un point-virgule (;)
8. des points de suspension (…)
9. des guillemets (« »)
10. une apostrophe (')

2 À vous de ponctuer! Listen to the following sentences and insert the punctuation marks you hear.

1. Voici ce que je dois acheter au marché des carottes des tomates et du fromage
2. Tu n'as pas encore commencé tes devoirs Tu vas peut-être les faire cette nuit
3. Monsieur Grosjean euh m'avez vous téléphoné
4. Ma sœur a répondu Je t'attends depuis deux heures et quart
5. Vous pouvez entrer Madame
6. Nous n'avons pas pu sortir hier soir il pleuvait trop fort

3 Dictée You will hear eight sentences. Each will be said twice. Listen carefully and write what you hear. Use abbreviations when you can.

1. _____
2. _____
3. _____
4. _____
5. _____
6. _____
7. _____
8. _____

ESPACE STRUCTURES

13A.1 Le futur simple with quand and dès que

1 **Conjuguez** Change each sentence from the present to the future. Repeat the correct response after the speaker. (6 *items*)

> **Modèle**
>
> Nous travaillons quand nous sommes prêts.
> **Nous travaillerons quand nous serons prêts.**

2 **Transformez** You will hear two sentences. Form a new sentence using **quand**. Repeat the correct response after the speaker. (6 *items*)

> **Modèle**
>
> Notre assistante vous dira. La réunion peut avoir lieu.
> **Notre assistante vous dira quand la réunion pourra avoir lieu.**

3 **Finissez** You will hear incomplete statements. Choose the correct ending for each statement.

1. a. quand il voit l'annonce.　　　　　b. quand il cherchera du travail.
2. a. quand elle aura plus d'expérience.　b. quand elle a un vrai métier.
3. a. nous appelons les candidats.　　　b. nous vous appellerons.
4. a. dès que ce stage a commencé.　　b. quand je ferai ce stage.
5. a. dès qu'il le faudra.　　　　　　　b. dès qu'on nous le demande.
6. a. dès que le téléphone a sonné.　　b. quand Mademoiselle Lefèvre ne sera pas là.

4 **Questions** Answer each question you hear using **dès que** and the cue in your lab manual. Repeat the correct response after the speaker.

> **Modèle**
>
> *You hear:* Quand est-ce que tu commenceras?
> *You see:* l'entreprise m'appelle
> *You say:* Je commencerai dès que l'entreprise m'appellera.

1. le stage commence
2. il est libre
3. quelqu'un décroche
4. l'annonce est dans le journal
5. cette compagnie le peut
6. il sort de son rendez-vous

13A.2 The interrogative pronoun lequel

1 **Identifiez** Listen to each statement and mark an X in the column of the form of **lequel** you hear.

> **Modèle**
>
> *You hear:* Desquels parlez-vous?
> *You mark:* an **X** under **desquels**

	lequel	laquelle	lesquels	duquel	desquels	auquel
Modèle	_____	_____	_____	_____	X	_____
1.	_____	_____	_____	_____	_____	_____
2.	_____	_____	_____	_____	_____	_____
3.	_____	_____	_____	_____	_____	_____
4.	_____	_____	_____	_____	_____	_____
5.	_____	_____	_____	_____	_____	_____
6.	_____	_____	_____	_____	_____	_____
7.	_____	_____	_____	_____	_____	_____
8.	_____	_____	_____	_____	_____	_____

2 **Transformez** Change each question to use a form of **lequel**. Repeat the correct question after the speaker. (*6 items*)

> **Modèle**
>
> Quel est ton candidat préféré? (candidat)
> *Lequel est ton préféré?*

1. (patron)   4. (candidate)
2. (entreprise)   5. (expérience)
3. (postes)   6. (numéro)

3 **Choisissez** Listen to each question and choose the most logical response.

1. a. Il a envoyé les lettres de motivation.
   b. Il les a envoyées.
2. a. J'y suis allé hier.
   b. Je suis allé au stage d'informatique.
3. a. Elle parle des deux derniers candidats.
   b. Elle parle des deux dernières candidates.
4. a. Je pense à leur projet d'été.
   b. Je pense partir.

5. a. Je veux appeler Carine.
   b. Je vais appeler avec son portable.
6. a. L'entreprise locale.
   b. Mon patron.
7. a. On peut assister à la formation de juin.
   b. On peut assister au stage de vente.
8. a. Nous allons répondre très vite.
   b. Nous allons répondre à l'annonce de Charles et Fils.

4 **Complétez** You will hear questions with a beep in place of the interrogative pronoun. Decide which form of **lequel** should complete each sentence. Repeat the correct question after the speaker. (*6 items*)

> **Modèle**
>
> Mon employé? *(beep)* penses-tu?
> *Mon employé? Auquel penses-tu?*

Unité 13

Leçon 13B

ESPACE CONTEXTES

---

1   **Identifiez** Listen to each description and then complete the sentence by identifying the person's occupation.

> **Modèle**
>
> *You hear:* Madame Cance travaille à la banque.
> *You write:* banquière

1. _____   5. _____

2. _____   6. _____

3. _____   7. _____

4. _____   8. _____

---

2   **Choisissez** Listen to each question and choose the most logical answer.

1. a. Non, il est client de notre banque.

     b. Non, il est agriculteur.

2. a. le mois prochain

     b. La réunion finira tard.

3. a. Oui, j'ai eu une augmentation.

     b. Oui, j'ai un emploi à mi-temps.

4. a. Non, ils sont au chômage.

     b. Oui, ils ont un bon salaire.

5. a. Non, elle va prendre un long congé.

     b. Non, elle est mal payée.

6. a. L'entreprise avait besoin d'ouvrières avec dix ans d'expérience.

     b. C'est une profession exigeante.

---

3   **Les professions** Listen to each statement and write the number of the statement below the photo it describes. There are more statements than there are photos.

a. _____   b. _____   c. _____   d. _____

LES SONS ET LES LETTRES

Les néologismes et le franglais

The use of words or neologisms of English origin in the French language is called **franglais**. These words often look identical to the English words, but they are pronounced like French words. Most of these words are masculine, and many end in **-ing**. Some of these words have long been accepted and used in French.

le sweat-shirt   le week-end   le shopping   le parking

Some words for foods and sports are very common, as are expressions in popular culture, business, and advertising.

un milk-shake   le base-ball   le top-modèle   le marketing

Many **franglais** words are recently coined terms (**néologismes**). These are common in contemporary fields, such as entertainment and technology. Some of these words do have French equivalents, but the **franglais** terms are used more often.

un e-mail = un courriel   le chat = la causette   une star = une vedette

Some **franglais** words do not exist in English at all, or they are used differently.

un brushing = _a blow-dry_   un relooking = _a makeover_   le zapping = _channel surfing_

1   **Prononcez** Répétez les mots suivants à voix haute.

1. flirter	4. le look	7. un scanneur	10. le shampooing
2. un fax	5. un clown	8. un CD-ROM	11. une speakerine
3. cliquer	6. le planning	9. le volley-ball	12. le chewing-gum

2   **Articulez** Répétez les phrases suivantes à voix haute.

1. Le cowboy porte un jean et un tee-shirt.
2. Julien joue au base-ball et il fait du footing.
3. J'ai envie d'un nouveau look, je vais faire du shopping.
4. Au snack-bar, je commande un hamburger, des chips et un milk-shake.
5. Tout ce qu'il veut faire, c'est rester devant la télé dans le living et zapper!

3   **Dictons** Répétez les dictons à voix haute.

1. Ce n'est pas la star qui fait l'audience, mais l'audience qui fait la star.
2. Un gentleman est un monsieur qui se sert d'une pince à sucre, même lorsqu'il est seul.

4   **Dictée** You will hear eight sentences. Each will be said twice. Listen carefully and write what you hear.

1. _____
2. _____
3. _____
4. _____
5. _____
6. _____
7. _____
8. _____

ESPACE STRUCTURES

13B.1 Si clauses

1 **Finissez** You will hear incomplete statements. Choose the correct ending for each statement.

1. a. si on le lui demandait.
   b. si c'est possible.

2. a. si elle demandait une augmentation.
   b. si nous faisons une réunion.

3. a. ils vont en Italie.
   b. ils auraient le temps de voyager.

4. a. je te le dirais tout de suite.
   b. tu pouvais essayer de postuler.

5. a. si le salaire reste élevé.
   b. si son mari n'était pas au chômage.

6. a. nous n'avons pas de syndicat.
   b. il y aurait moins de problèmes.

2 **Modifiez** Change each sentence you hear to form a **si** clause with the **imparfait**. Repeat the correct response after the speaker. (6 *items*)

> _Modèle_
>
> On va au bureau ensemble?
> Si on allait au bureau ensemble?

3 **Questions** Answer each question you hear using the cue in your lab manual. Repeat the correct response after the speaker. (6 *items*)

> _Modèle_
>
> _You hear:_ Qu'est-ce que tu feras s'il fait beau demain?
> _You see:_ marcher jusqu'au bureau
> _You say:_ S'il fait beau demain, je marcherai jusqu'au bureau.

1. aller au cinéma
2. nous donner une augmentation
3. organiser une réunion
4. faire la fête
5. partir en vacances
6. continuer à travailler pour leur entreprise

4 **Transformez** Change each sentence to a speculation or hypothesis. Repeat the correct response after the speaker. (6 *items*)

> _Modèle_
>
> Si nous embauchons quelqu'un, nous devrons en parler au chef du personnel.
> Si nous embauchions quelqu'un, nous devrions en parler au chef du personnel.

13B.2 Relative pronouns qui, que, dont, où

1 **Identifiez** Listen to each statement and mark an **X** in the column of the relative pronoun you hear.

> *You hear:* Vous n'aurez pas l'augmentation dont vous rêvez.
> *You mark:* an **X** under **dont**

	qui	que	dont	où
Modèle	_____	_____	X	_____
1.	_____	_____	_____	_____
2.	_____	_____	_____	_____
3.	_____	_____	_____	_____
4.	_____	_____	_____	_____
5.	_____	_____	_____	_____
6.	_____	_____	_____	_____
7.	_____	_____	_____	_____
8.	_____	_____	_____	_____

2 **Finissez** You will hear incomplete sentences. Choose the correct ending for each one.

1. a. admire beaucoup les autres.   b. j'admire beaucoup.
2. a. le prof nous a parlé?   b. a parlé du prof?
3. a. me permet de travailler à la maison.   b. j'aime beaucoup.
4. a. est la salle de réunion?   b. je travaille, je prends ma voiture.
5. a. on rêve est celle d'artiste.   b. je laisse un message.
6. a. aide les humains aussi.   b. on aime beaucoup.

3 **Complétez** Listen to Annette talk about her job search and write the missing relative pronouns in your lab manual.

Le métier (1) _____ j'ai choisi, c'est celui de psychologue pour animaux. Eh bien, je ne trouvais

pas de patients (2) _____ pouvaient être réguliers. Alors, j'ai décidé de chercher du travail

temporaire. L'endroit (3) _____ je voulais travailler était une clinique vétérinaire. La formation

(4) _____ j'ai faite à l'université peut me servir dans une clinique. J'ai donc téléphoné à une

clinique (5) _____ j'emmène d'habitude mon chat pour des visites vétérinaires. J'ai parlé avec

le docteur (6) _____ était très gentil et on a pris rendez-vous pour un entretien. On y a parlé de

ma formation et de mes expériences professionnelles. Ce (7) _____ on a parlé lui a beaucoup

plu (*made him happy*) et il m'a embauchée sur place, comme assistante. Maintenant, je peux exercer ma

profession de temps en temps quand il y a un animal (8) _____ est stressé.

4 **Transformez** You will hear two sentences. Form a new sentence using a relative pronoun. Repeat the correct answer after the speaker. (*6 items*)

> Je cherche un travail. Ce travail offre une assurance-maladie.
> *Je cherche un travail qui offre une assurance-maladie.*

Unité 14

ESPACE CONTEXTES

1   **Identifiez** You will hear a series of words. Write the word that does not belong in each series.

1. _____   5. _____

2. _____   6. _____

3. _____   7. _____

4. _____   8. _____

2   **Choisissez** Listen to each question and choose the most logical response.

1. a. Oui, les usines polluent.   b. Oui, les voitures sont un danger pour l'environnement.

2. a. C'est pour éviter le gaspillage.   b. Oui, il est utile.

3. a. Parce que l'eau, c'est la vie.   b. Parce qu'il faut proposer des solutions.

4. a. La pluie acide.   b. L'accident à la centrale.

5. a. Deux fois par semaine.   b. À cause de la surpopulation.

6. a. Non, nous n'avons pas d'espace.   b. Oui, il y en a souvent ici.

3   **Décrivez** Look at the picture in your lab manual. Listen to these statements and decide whether each statement is **vrai** or **faux**.

	Vrai	Faux			Vrai	Faux
1.	○	○		4.	○	○
2.	○	○		5.	○	○
3.	○	○		6.	○	○

French and English spelling

You have seen that many French words only differ slightly from their English counterparts. Many differ in predictable ways. English words that end in *-y* often end in **-ie** in French.

    biolog**ie**   psycholog**ie**   énerg**ie**   écolog**ie**

English words that end in *-ity* often end in **-ité** in French.

    qualit**é**   universit**é**   cit**é**   nationalit**é**

French equivalents of English words that end in *-ist* often end in **-iste**.

    art**iste**   optim**iste**   pessim**iste**   dent**iste**

French equivalents of English words that end in *-or* and *-er* often end in **-eur**. This tendency is especially common for words that refer to people.

    doct**eur**   act**eur**   employ**eur**   agricult**eur**

Other English words that end in *-er* end in **-re** in French.

    cent**re**   memb**re**   lit**re**   théât**re**

Other French words vary in ways that are less predictable, but they are still easy to recognize.

    problème   orchestre   carotte   calculatrice

1   **Prononcez** Répétez les mots suivants à voix haute.

1. tigre
2. bleu
3. lettre
4. salade
5. poème
6. banane
7. tourisme
8. moniteur
9. pharmacie
10. écologiste
11. conducteur
12. anthropologie

2   **Articulez** Répétez les phrases suivantes à voix haute.

1. Ma cousine est vétérinaire.
2. Le moteur ne fonctionne pas.
3. À la banque, Carole paie par chèque.
4. Mon oncle écrit l'adresse sur l'enveloppe.
5. À la station-service, le mécanicien a réparé le moteur.

3   **Dictons** Répétez les dictons à voix haute.

1. On reconnaît l'arbre à son fruit.
2. On ne fait pas d'omelette sans casser des œufs.

4   **Dictée** You will hear eight sentences. Each will be said twice. Listen carefully and write what you hear.

1. _____
2. _____
3. _____
4. _____
5. _____
6. _____
7. _____
8. _____

14A.1 Demonstrative pronouns

1 **En vacances** Listen to each statement and write its number below the drawing it describes. There are more statements than there are drawings.

a. _____   b. _____   c. _____

d. _____   e. _____

2 **Transformez** Change each statement to use a demonstrative pronoun. Repeat the correct response after the speaker. (*6 items*)

> **Modèle**
> La pollution de l'eau est aussi grave que la pollution des villes.
> *La pollution de l'eau est aussi grave que celle des villes.*

3 **Logique ou illogique?** Listen to these statements and indicate whether they are **logique** or illogique.

	Logique	Illogique			Logique	Illogique
1.	O	O		5.	O	O
2.	O	O		6.	O	O
3.	O	O		7.	O	O
4.	O	O		8.	O	O

4 **Questions** Answer each question you hear using the cue in your lab manual and the appropriate demonstrative pronoun. Repeat the correct response after the speaker.

> **Modèle**
> *You hear:* Quel emballage est-ce que nous devons utiliser?
> *You see:* l'emballage qui ferme le mieux
> *You say:* Celui qui ferme le mieux.

1. les sacs qui se recyclent
2. le problème du réchauffement de la planète
3. mes amis qui sont les plus optimistes
4. les solutions qui ont l'air trop compliquées et les solutions qui coûtent cher
5. l'avenir qu'on prépare aujourd'hui
6. les questions qui sont simples

14A.2 The subjunctive (Part 1): introduction, regular verbs, and impersonal expressions

1 **Choisissez** You will hear some sentences with a beep in place of a verb. Decide which verb should complete each sentence and circle it.

> **Modèle**
> *You hear:* Il est impossible que ce gaspillage *(beep)*
> *You see:* continue   continuait
> *You circle:* continue

1. abolissions   abolissons
2. aidez   aidiez
3. connaissent   connaîtraient
4. travaillent   travaillaient
5. intéressons   intéressions
6. arrêtaient   arrêtent
7. interdise   interdit
8. proposiez   proposez

2 **Conjuguez** Form a new sentence using the cue you hear as the subject. Repeat the correct response after the speaker. (*6 items*)

> **Modèle**
> Est-ce qu'il faut que je recycle ces emballages? (nous)
> *Est-ce qu'il faut que nous recyclions ces emballages?*

3 **Transformez** Change each sentence you hear to the present subjunctive using the expressions you see in your lab manual. Repeat the correct response after the speaker.

> **Modèle**
> *You hear:* Tu recycleras ces bouteilles.
> *You see:* Il est important...
> *You say:* Il est important que tu recycles ces bouteilles.

1. Il n'est pas essentiel...
2. Il est bon...
3. Il est important...
4. Il est dommage...
5. Il ne faut pas...
6. Il vaut mieux...

4 **Complétez** Listen to what Manu wants to do to save the environment and write the missing words in your lab manual.

Il faut que nous (1) _____ notre quotidien. Il vaut mieux que nous (2) _____ d'utiliser des sacs en plastique et il est important que les gens (3) _____ à recycler chez eux! Il est essentiel aussi que nous n' (4) _____ plus de produits ménagers dangereux; il est bon qu'on (5) _____ des produits plus naturels. Enfin, il est nécessaire que nous (6) _____ tous de ne pas gaspiller l'électricité, car il est impossible que les pays (7) _____ à développer l'énergie nucléaire. Avec ces simples idées, il est très possible que nous (8) _____ à sauver la planète!

Unité 14

ESPACE CONTEXTES

Leçon 14B

1   Associez Circle the words that are logically associated with each word you hear.

1. chasser   détruire   préserver
2. désert   rivière   lac
3. promenade   marche   autoroute
4. champ   bois   forêt
5. étoile   champ   falaise
6. montagne   chasse   extinction

2   Logique ou illogique? Listen to these statements and indicate whether they are **logique** or **illogique**.

	Logique	Illogique			Logique	Illogique
1.	○	○		5.	○	○
2.	○	○		6.	○	○
3.	○	○		7.	○	○
4.	○	○		8.	○	○

3   Décrivez Look at the picture in your lab manual. Listen to these statements and decide whether each statement is **vrai** or **faux**.

	Vrai	Faux
1.	○	○
2.	○	○
3.	○	○
4.	○	○
5.	○	○
6.	○	○

LES SONS ET LES LETTRES

Homophones

Many French words sound alike, but are spelled differently. As you have already learned, sometimes the only difference between two words is a diacritical mark. Other words that sound alike have more obvious differences in spelling.

| a / **à** | ou / **où** | sont / son | en / an |

Several forms of a single verb may sound alike. To tell which form is being used, listen for the subject or words that indicate tense.

| je **parle** | tu **parles** | ils **parlent** |
| vous **parlez** | j'ai **parlé** | je vais **parler** |

Many words that sound alike are different parts of speech. Use context to tell them apart.

VERB	POSSESSIVE ADJECTIVE	PREPOSITION	NOUN
Ils **sont** belges.	C'est **son** mari.	Tu vas **en** France?	Il a un **an**.

You may encounter multiple spellings of words that sound alike. Again, context is the key to understanding which word is being used.

je **peux** _I can_	elle **peut** _she can_	**peu** _a little, few_
le **foie** _the liver_	la **foi** _faith_	une **fois** _one time_
haut _high_	l'**eau** _water_	**au** _at, to, in the_

1 **Prononcez** Répétez les paires de mots suivantes à voix haute.

1. ce	se	4. foi	fois	7. au	eau	10. lis	lit
2. leur	leurs	5. ces	ses	8. peut	peu	11. quelle	qu'elle
3. né	nez	6. vert	verre	9. où	ou	12. c'est	s'est

2 **Choisissez** Choisissez le mot qui convient à chaque phrase.

1. Je (lis / lit) le journal tous les jours.
2. Son chien est sous le (lis / lit).
3. Corinne est (née / nez) à Paris.
4. Elle a mal au (née / nez).

3 **Jeux de mots** Répétez les jeux de mots à voix haute.

1. Le ver vert va vers le verre.
2. Mon père est maire, mon frère est masseur.

4 **Dictée** You will hear eight sentences. Each will be said twice. Listen carefully and write what you hear.

1. _____
2. _____
3. _____
4. _____
5. _____
6. _____
7. _____
8. _____

ESPACE STRUCTURES

14B.1 The subjunctive (Part 2): will and emotion, irregular subjunctive forms

1 **Identifiez** Listen to each sentence and write the infinitive of the subjunctive verb you hear.

> **Modèle**
>
> *You hear:* Je veux que tu regardes la Lune ce soir.
> *You write:* regarder

1. _____   4. _____

2. _____   5. _____

3. _____   6. _____

2 **Conjuguez** Form a new sentence using the cue you hear as the subject of the verb in the subjunctive. Repeat the correct response after the speaker. (*6 items*)

> **Modèle**
>
> J'aimerais que tu fasses attention. (vous)
> J'aimerais que *vous fassiez attention.*

3 **Associez** Listen to each statement and write its number below the drawing it describes. There are more statements than there are drawings.

a. _____   b. _____   c. _____

d. _____   e. _____   f. _____

4 **Les conseils** Listen to Julien give advice to his sons. Then read the statements in your lab manual and decide whether they are **vrai** or **faux**.

	Vrai	Faux
1. Julien exige que ses fils soient prudents.	○	○
2. Il veut qu'ils aient froid.	○	○
3. Il ne recommande pas qu'ils utilisent des cartes.	○	○
4. Il préférerait qu'ils aient un téléphone.	○	○
5. Il aimerait qu'ils prennent des photos.	○	○

14B.2 Comparatives and superlatives of nouns

1 **Identifiez** Listen to each statement and mark an **X** in the column of the comparative or superlative you hear.

Modèle

You hear: La France a beaucoup plus de rivières
que de fleuves.
You mark: an **X** under **plus de**

	moins de	plus de	autant de	le plus de	le moins de
Modèle	_____	X	_____	_____	_____
1.	_____	_____	_____	_____	_____
2.	_____	_____	_____	_____	_____
3.	_____	_____	_____	_____	_____
4.	_____	_____	_____	_____	_____
5.	_____	_____	_____	_____	_____
6.	_____	_____	_____	_____	_____
7.	_____	_____	_____	_____	_____
8.	_____	_____	_____	_____	_____

2 **Changez** Change each sentence you hear to say that the opposite is true. Repeat the correct response after the speaker. (*6 items*)

Modèle

Il y a plus d'écureuils en France qu'en Amérique du Nord.
Il y a moins d'écureuils en France qu'en Amérique du Nord.

3 **Choisissez** Listen to each question and choose the most logical response.

1. a. Elles ont plus d'étoiles.
2. a. J'ai moins mal et j'ai plus d'énergie.
3. a. Il n'y a pas autant de circulation en ville.
4. a. Il n'a pas autant d'herbe.
5. a. Ils ont plus de problèmes que nous.
6. a. Le parc a autant de serpents que de vaches.

b. Il y a moins d'arbres.
b. Cette ville a plus de pharmacies que de cafés.
b. Elle a autant de plages que de montagnes.
b. Nous avons aperçu plus d'arbres que de lapins.
b. Ils ont moins de lois contre la pollution.
b. Encore plus d'espèces sont menacées.

4 **Écoutez** Listen to the conversation and correct these statements.

1. Il y a moins d'animaux dans le parc.

_____

2. Il y a autant d'endroits à explorer dans le parc.

_____

3. Le parc a moins de touristes en cette saison.

_____

4. Les volcans ont autant de charme.

_____

5. Il y a plus de pierres pour sa collection dans le parc.

_____

6. Il y a plus d'herbe dans le parc.

_____

Unité 15

ESPACE CONTEXTES

---

1 **Les définitions** You will hear some definitions. Write the letter of the word being defined.

_____ 1.   a. un réalisateur

_____ 2.   b. une troupe

_____ 3.   c. des applaudissements

_____ 4.   d. un musicien

_____ 5.   e. un spectateur

_____ 6.   f. un orchestre

_____ 7.   g. une comédie

_____ 8.   h. une chanteuse

---

2 **Associez** Circle the words that are not logically associated with each word you hear.

1. séance	chœur	opéra
2. genre	pièce de théâtre	gratuit
3. pièce de théâtre	réalisatrice	joueur de batterie
4. début	fin	place
5. dramaturge	chansons	comédie musicale
6. danseurs	compositeur	acteurs

---

3 **Les artistes** Listen to each statement and write its number below the illustration it describes. There are more statements than there are illustrations.

a. _____   b. _____   c. _____

LES SONS ET LES LETTRES

Les liaisons obligatoires et les liaisons interdites

Rules for making liaisons are complex, and have many exceptions. Generally, a liaison is made between pronouns, and between a pronoun and a verb that begins with a vowel or vowel sound.

    vous en avez   nous habitons   ils aiment   elles arrivent

Make liaisons between articles, numbers, or the verb **est** and a noun or adjective that begins with a vowel or a vowel sound.

    un éléphant   les amis   di**x** hommes   Roger est enchanté.

There is a liaison after many single-syllable adverbs, conjunctions, and prepositions.

    très intéressant   chez eux   quan**d** elle   quan**d** on décidera

Many expressions have obligatory liaisons that may or may not follow these rules.

    C'est-à-dire...   Comment allez-vous?   plus ou moins   avant-hier

Never make a liaison before or after the conjunction **et** or between a noun and a verb that follows it. Likewise, do not make a liaison between a singular noun and an adjective that follows it.

    un garçon et une fille   Gilbert adore le football.   un cours intéressant

There is no liaison before **h aspiré** or before the word **oui** and before numbers.

    un hamburger   les héros   un oui et un non   mes onze animaux

---

1 **Prononcez** Répétez les mots suivants à voix haute.

    1. les héros   2. mon petit ami   3. un pays africain   4. les onze étages

---

2 **Articulez** Répétez les phrases suivantes à voix haute.

    1. Ils en veulent onze.   3. Christelle et Albert habitent en Angleterre.

    2. Vous vous êtes bien amusés hier soir?   4. Quand est-ce que Charles a acheté ces objets?

---

3 **Dictons** Répétez les dictons à voix haute.

    1. Deux avis valent mieux qu'un.   2. Les murs ont des oreilles.

---

4 **Dictée** You will hear eight sentences. Each will be said twice. Listen carefully and write what you hear.

    1. _____

    2. _____

    3. _____

    4. _____

    5. _____

    6. _____

    7. _____

    8. _____

ESPACE STRUCTURES

15A.1 The subjunctive (Part 3): verbs of doubt, disbelief, and uncertainty; more irregular subjunctive forms

1   **Identifiez** Listen to each statement in the subjunctive and mark an **X** in the column of the verb you hear.

> **Modèle**
>
> *You hear:* Il est impossible qu'ils aillent au théâtre ce soir.
> *You mark:* an **X** under **aller**

	aller	pouvoir	savoir	vouloir
Modèle	X			
1.				
2.				
3.				
4.				
5.				
6.				
7.				
8.				

2   **Transformez** Change each sentence you hear to the subjunctive using the expressions you see in your lab manual. Repeat the correct response after the speaker.

> **Modèle**
>
> *You hear:* Il peut présenter le metteur en scène ce soir.
> *You see:* Il n'est pas certain que...
> *You say:* Il n'est pas certain qu'il puisse présenter le metteur en scène ce soir.

1. Il est impossible que...
2. Mes amis ne pensent pas que...
3. Il n'est pas vrai que...
4. Je ne suis pas sûr que...
5. Le metteur en scène doute que...
6. Il n'est pas certain que...

3   **Choisissez** Listen to each sentence and decide whether the second verb is in the indicative or in the subjunctive.

1. a. indicatif   b. subjonctif   5. a. indicatif   b. subjonctif
2. a. indicatif   b. subjonctif   6. a. indicatif   b. subjonctif
3. a. indicatif   b. subjonctif   7. a. indicatif   b. subjonctif
4. a. indicatif   b. subjonctif   8. a. indicatif   b. subjonctif

4   **Le critique de film** Listen to this movie critic. Then, answer the questions in your lab manual.

1. De quoi le critique doute-t-il? _____
2. Que pense-t-il du réalisateur? _____
3. Qu'est-ce qui est impossible à son avis? _____
4. Que dit-il de l'acteur principal? _____
5. Comment trouve-t-il le film? _____

15A.2 Possessive pronouns

1 **Identifiez** You will hear sentences with possessive pronouns. Decide which thing the possessive pronoun in each sentence is referring to.

1. a. mon portable   b. ma calculatrice
2. a. notre maison   b. nos voitures
3. a. ton sac à dos   b. tes lunettes de soleil
4. a. leur fils   b. leur fille
5. a. vos parents   b. votre mère
6. a. leur ordinateur   b. leur télévision

2 **Transformez** You will hear sentences that sound a little repetitive. Improve each sentence by changing the second possessive adjective and noun into a possessive pronoun. Repeat the correct answer after the speaker. (*6 items*)

> **Modèle**
>
> Tu as ton appareil photo et j'ai mon appareil photo aussi.
> **Tu as *ton appareil photo* et j'ai le mien aussi.**

3 **Complétez** Listen to Faïza talk about her social life. You will hear beeps where the possessive pronouns should be. Write the missing possessive pronouns in your lab manual.

Vous avez un cercle d'amis? Eh bien, j'ai beaucoup d'amis. (1) _____ est très grand!

Qu'est-ce que vos amis et vous aimez faire pour vous amuser? (2) _____ vont souvent en

ville. On se promène, on prend des repas pas trop chers au petit bistro du coin, on regarde un film ou

un spectacle si on a un peu d'argent... La mère de Juliette n'aime pas qu'on rentre après 23h00, mais

(3) _____ me permet de rentrer assez tard si je suis avec des amis qu'elle connaît. Le père de

Slimane est très stricte et il ne sort pas souvent avec nous parce qu'il doit souvent travailler à la maison.

Mais Stéphane sort tous les soirs parce que (4) _____ n'est pas stricte du tout! Vos amies,

quand elles sortent entre elles le soir sans les garçons, est-ce qu'elles font un peu attention pour ne pas

avoir de problèmes? C'est le cas pour (5) _____. Elles sont intelligentes. Maintenant que vous

connaissez un peu plus mon cercle d'amis, j'aimerais bien connaître (6) _____.

4 **Modifiez** You will hear a series of sentences. Rewrite them, replacing the possessive adjective and noun with a possessive pronoun.

> **Modèle**
>
> *You hear:* C'est ma guitare.
> *You write:* C'est la mienne.

1. _____   4. _____
2. _____   5. _____
3. _____   6. _____

Unité 15

ESPACE CONTEXTES

---

1   **Logique ou illogique?** Listen to these statements and indicate whether they are **logique** or **illogique**.

	Logique	Illogique			Logique	Illogique
1.	O	O		5.	O	O
2.	O	O		6.	O	O
3.	O	O		7.	O	O
4.	O	O		8.	O	O

---

2   **Décrivez** For each drawing, you will hear two statements. Choose the one that corresponds to the drawing.

1. a.   b.   2. a.   b.   3. a.   b.

---

3   **Le programme** Listen to this announcement about tonight's TV program. Then, answer the questions in your lab manual.

1. À quelle heure on peut voir les infos?

_____

2. Comment s'appelle le jeu télévisé?

_____

3. Quelle est l'histoire du drame psychologique?

_____

4. Qu'est-ce que «Des vies et des couleurs»?

_____

5. Qui est l'invité du magazine?

_____

6. Est-ce qu'Éric Bernier n'est que chanteur?

_____

LES SONS ET LES LETTRES

Les abréviations

French speakers use many acronyms. This is especially true in newspapers, televised news programs, and in political discussions. Many stand for official organizations or large companies.

EDF = Électricité de France   **ONU** = Organisation des Nations Unies

People often use acronyms when referring to geographical place names and transportation.

É-U = États-Unis   **RF** = République Française

RN = Route Nationale   **TGV** = Train à Grande Vitesse

Many are simply shortened versions of common expressions or compound words.

SVP = S'il Vous Plaît   **RV** = Rendez-Vous   **RDC** = Rez-De-Chaussée

When speaking, some acronyms are spelled out, while others are pronounced like any other word.

CEDEX = Courrier d'Entreprise à Distribution Exceptionnelle *(an overnight delivery service)*

---

1 Prononcez Répétez les abréviations suivantes à voix haute.

1. W-C = Water-Closet
2. HS = Hors Service *(out of order)*
3. VF = Version Française
4. CV = Curriculum Vitæ
5. TVA = Taxe à la Valeur Ajoutée *(added)*

6. DELF = Diplôme d'Études en Langue Française
7. RATP = Régie Autonome *(independent administration)* des Transports Parisiens
8. SMIC = Salaire Minimum Interprofessionnel de Croissance *(growth)*

---

2 Assortissez-les Répétez les abréviations à voix haute. Que représentent-elles?

____ 1. ECP
____ 2. GDF
____ 3. DEUG
____ 4. TTC
____ 5. PDG
____ 6. OVNI

a. objet volant non identifié
b. toutes taxes comprises
c. président-directeur général
d. école centrale de Paris
e. gaz de France
f. diplôme d'études universitaires générales

---

3 Expressions Répétez les expressions à voix haute.

1. RSVP (Répondez, S'il Vous Plaît).
2. Elle est BCBG (Bon Chic, Bon Genre).

---

4 Dictée You will hear eight sentences. Each will be said twice. Listen carefully and write what you hear.

1. _____
2. _____
3. _____
4. _____
5. _____
6. _____
7. _____
8. _____

ESPACE STRUCTURES

15B.1 The subjunctive (Part 4): the subjunctive with conjunctions

1 **Identifiez** Listen to each statement and mark an **X** in the column of the conjunction you hear.

> **Modèle**
>
> *You hear:* Nous n'y arriverons pas sans que vous
>   fassiez un effort.
> *You mark:* an **X** under **sans que**

	sans que	sans	avant que	avant de	pour que	pour
Modèle	X	____	____	____	____	____
1.	____	____	____	____	____	____
2.	____	____	____	____	____	____
3.	____	____	____	____	____	____
4.	____	____	____	____	____	____
5.	____	____	____	____	____	____
6.	____	____	____	____	____	____
7.	____	____	____	____	____	____
8.	____	____	____	____	____	____

2 **Finissez** You will hear incomplete sentences. Choose the correct ending for each sentence.

1. a. jusqu'à ce qu'il trouve son style. b. avant qu'il regarde un jeu télévisé.
2. a. à condition que les enfants ne soient pas là. b. à moins que nous regarderons la télé.
3. a. avant que le conte finisse mal. b. à moins que tu sois toujours malade.
4. a. pour que les critiques en parlent. b. à moins qu'il y ait un temps
                                             catastrophique à annoncer
5. a. avant qu'elle m'explique la vie de son auteur. b. à condition que le magazine fasse un article.
6. a. pour que l'histoire soit populaire. b. à condition qu'il finisse bien.

3 **Conjuguez** Form a new sentence using the cue you hear as the subject of the first verb. Repeat the correct response after the speaker. (*6 items*)

> **Modèle**
>
> Tu ne partiras pas sans finir ton assiette. (nous)
> *Nous ne partirons pas sans que tu finisses ton assiette.*

4 **Décrivez** Listen to each statement and write its number below the drawing it describes. There are more statements than there are drawings.

a. _____ b. _____ c. _____ d. _____

15B.2 Review of the subjunctive

1 **Choisissez** Listen to each sentence and decide whether you hear a verb in the subjunctive.

	Subjonctif	Pas de subjonctif		Subjonctif	Pas de subjonctif
1.	○	○	5.	○	○
2.	○	○	6.	○	○
3.	○	○	7.	○	○
4.	○	○	8.	○	○

2 **Complétez** You will hear sentences with a beep in place of a verb. Decide which verb should complete each sentence and circle it. Repeat the correct response after the speaker.

> **Modèle**
> *You hear:* Cette artiste sera douée à condition que
> vous lui *(beep)* des conseils.
> *You see:* donnez   donniez
> *You circle:* donniez

1.	apprennent	apprendront	5.	soit	est
2.	sont	soient	6.	devenir	devienne
3.	arrêtez	arrêtiez	7.	aiment	aime
4.	lisions	lire	8.	invitions	invitons

3 **Transformez** Change each sentence you hear to the subjunctive using the expressions you see in your lab manual. Repeat the correct response after the speaker.

> **Modèle**
> *You hear:* Elle vend beaucoup de tableaux.
> *You see:* Je doute que...
> *You say:* Je doute qu'elle vende beaucoup de tableaux.

1. Il n'est pas essentiel que...
2. Monsieur Bétan ne croit pas que...
3. On essaiera de voir la pièce à moins que...
4. Il est dommage que...
5. Est-ce que tu es triste...
6. Il vaut mieux que...

4 **Le professionnel** Listen to the trainer's advice. Then, number the drawings in your lab manual in the correct order.

a. _____ b. _____ c. _____

d. _____ e. _____